William Jolly

Ruskin on Education

Some needed but neglected elements

William Jolly

Ruskin on Education
Some needed but neglected elements

ISBN/EAN: 9783337219390

Printed in Europe, USA, Canada, Australia, Japan

Cover: Foto ©Suzi / pixelio.de

More available books at **www.hansebooks.com**

RUSKIN ON EDUCATION

RUSKIN ON EDUCATION

SOME NEEDED BUT NEGLECTED ELEMENTS

RESTATED AND REVIEWED

BY

WILLIAM JOLLY

LONDON
GEORGE ALLEN, 156, CHARING CROSS ROAD
AND AT ORPINGTON
1894
[*All rights reserved*]

PREFACE

One of the most reassuring signs of the times, in this over-pushing but progressive age, is the great and growing interest manifested by all classes in the Education of the young. Remarkable, if not in many respects surprising, as have been the improvements in this all-important subject during the century, especially since the passing of the Education Acts of 1870 and 1872, our views in regard to it still urgently require enlightenment. Our present system sadly needs broadening, deepening, and elevating, in both purpose and process, more than even most experts have yet perceived or imagined.

Of men to point the way towards desirable reform, there is no one whose views should be more potential for this end than

John Ruskin. This is true of his work in Education as much as in other departments of his varied activity, in spite of existing popular and scholastic opinion in regard to his ideas. This opinion is mainly based on ignorance of the man and his views; on prejudice—both in its common acceptation and in its literal meaning of pre-judgment, condemnation without adequate examination; on the too ready acceptance of erroneous criticism, by the mass of the people, even by the more thoughtful among them; and, as he himself has told us, on the narrowing and intolerant pursuit of less worthy aims in this mammon-loving, competitive time, whose din and dust have drowned and darkened the brightest and wisest thoughts of one of the greatest prophets and preachers of our day.

In connection with Education, in spite of the facts being far otherwise, Ruskin has generally been thought to have written little, and done less, than in many other better known fields; and that little is almost universally considered to be of more extreme and eccentric type than is usual even with this unconventional critic and philosopher. At best, his views are deemed by not a few of the more enlightened of his students as " counsels of perfection." They are certainly all this, in its truest sense, and, if listened to and acted on, would lead us, more rapidly than we have yet gone, towards the perfection which does not exist in such an advancing Science and Art as Education, of whose future developments, however, Ruskin's suggestions form a bright and encouraging vision.

The present work is a brief and partial attempt to prove this position in regard to Ruskin; by rendering more accessible and popular some of his more pregnant views regarding certain primary and pressing defects in our educational practice, than has yet been possible amid his scattered and multitudinous utterances.

Portions of the wide educational field traversed by him, I have as yet been prevented by want of time and health from overtaking—such as, the all-important and rising function of Physical Education, now, happily, more acknowledged; the wide and ever-extending range of Intellectual Education, on which his views are advanced and valuable; and Mr. Ruskin's own practical attempts at a broader and worthier training than is yet common, which are both interesting and instructive. For these, I would at present refer those interested to the invaluable Bibliography of his works; the index to "Fors Clavigera"; Collingwood's "Life and Work of John Ruskin" (Methuen & Co., 1893); "Studies in Ruskin," by Edward T. Cook (George Allen, 1890); and "John Ruskin: his Life and Teaching," by J. Marshall Mather (third edition, 1890; Frederick Warne & Co.).

This book is the outcome of former expositions of Ruskin's views and their relations to those of other educationists, given by me from time to time: in lectures delivered to the Glasgow Ruskin Society, as President, and to the teachers of my own district, as H.M. Inspector of Schools; in a series of articles in the weekly journal,

Great Thoughts, of which this issue is mainly a reprint; and in notes buried in Educational Blue Books, which are little read even by the few whose business or studies lead them there, and are neglected by all others.

Not the least matter for personal gratification is the fact, that its present publication was arranged for, unsolicited, by Mr. Allen, whose name is so honourably identified with the artistic production of the Great Master's works.

CONTENTS

PART FIRST

THE GENERAL PRINCIPLES OF EDUCATION

RUSKIN'S RELATIONS TO EDUCATION—

                                                                                    PAGE

  I. Ruskin's Views on Education should be better known. 3
  II. His Study of Education was Philanthropic . 4
  III. His Opinion of Education as it is . . . 7
  IV. His Ideas of what Education should·be . . 11

SOME GENERAL PRINCIPLES OF EDUCATION ACCORDING TO RUSKIN—

  I. Education should be regulated by Natural Endowment 12
    The Means of discovering it 13
  II. Education should not be conducted with a view to mere "Success in Life" . . . 15
    It should aim at Real Advancement in Living 17
  III. Education should train to Useful Work . . 20
    The kind of work needed 23

	PAGE
Its effects on Religion	24
Its relation to Physical Exercise	26
The growth of this idea in Schools	28
IV. Education should not be estimated by the mere Acquisition of Knowledge	32
V. The importance of the world of Nature in Education	36
The out-door class-room	41
VI. Our educational standard should not be too high	45
VII. Education should vary with circumstances	48
VIII. The prevalent estimate of "the Three R's" is erroneous	50
Ruskin's central position in regard to them	55
The importance of Ruskin's views	58
Our existing Educational Ideal low and defective	61

PART SECOND

THE TRAINING OF TASTE IN SCHOOLS

I. THE NEED FOR CULTIVATING TASTE IN SCHOOLS	64
The Nature of Taste	66
The chief groups of the Æsthetic Arts	67
How much may be essayed in the Cultivation of Taste	68
The vital importance of Childhood in its training	69

CONTENTS xiii

	PAGE
The importance of the School-room for this training	72
Our Schools devoid of Taste in the past	74
The Two ways of training Taste in School	75
Schools should be refined in Architecture and Decoration	76
The Views of Ancient thinkers	78
Æsthetic Education in Athens	80
The Views of Montaigne and Fenelon	81
Other Opinions Coincident	83

II. WHAT HAS BEEN DONE TOWARDS THE REALISATION OF THESE PRINCIPLES . . 85
  The beginning of an Æsthetic Revival . . 86

III. THE MEANS OF ÆSTHETIC CULTIVATION IN SCHOOLS 87
  1. Scholastic diagrams 87
  2. Special æsthetic decorations . . . 88
  3. Illustrations in school books . . . 90
  4. Plants and flowers 91
  5. The study of external nature . . . 92
    A New Crusade in favour of training through Nature needed . . . 93
  6. Other elements in æsthetic training . . 95

IV. THE MORAL EFFECTS OF ÆSTHETIC CULTURE 96
  What should be done ? 97
  Recent encouraging progress 98

PART THIRD

MORAL EDUCATION IN SCHOOLS

	PAGE
MORALITY A CONSTANT ELEMENT IN ALL RUSKIN'S TEACHING	100
I. The present conduct of Moral Education unsatisfactory	101
Ruskin's condemnation of it	102
The Need of better Moral Training	104
II. The Teaching should be Systematic	105
III. Moral Training Paramount and First	106
The Real End of Education is Moral	107
Ruskin's Summary of its aims	108
Intellectual and Moral Education contrasted by Ruskin	109
Herbart's Testimony	111
IV. The Subject-matter of Systematic Moral teaching	112
The Chief Duties to be taught	115
Ruskin's exposition of these	116
V. How to accomplish these Moral aims	118
VI. Virtues on which Ruskin lays stress	119
1. Cleanliness	119
2. Obedience	120
3. Kindness to animal life	120
4. Honesty	121
VII. Virtues specially emphasised by Ruskin	123
1. Intellectual and Social humility	124
Illustration from his own School Days	126

CONTENTS

	PAGE
2. Reverent admiration.	127
3. Emulation condemned	130
No Competition to be allowed	131
The true purpose of Examinations.	133
How should Emulation be used?	134
VIII. Education should teach the true meaning of Wealth.	135
Our estimate of Wealth generally wrong	136
In what true Wealth consists	136
Education should furnish a child with a Plan of Life.	138
The views of several educationists	138
Ruskin's views	140
The editor's views	143
IX. The teaching of Social and Political Economy	145
Its past neglect	146
Ruskin's Political Economy.	147
William Ellis's work in this educational field	147
The subject begins to be recognised	150
X. The Systematic teaching of Moral Duty should be universal	151
The Means of doing it.	152
The Influence of such teaching	153
It is partially recognised by the Education Department.	154
It should be extended and Systematically taught	155
Text-books for the teaching of the subject	155

	PAGE
XI. Auxiliary aids to Moral Training in school	157
1. Poetry for Recitation	158
Music Pieces to be Avoided	158
Pieces to be Selected	160
2. Pieces for Music	161
Convivial Songs to be Avoided	162
Love Songs Objectionable	163
XII. The Relation of Moral Training to Religious Instruction	165
The General Teaching of Moral Duty is surely now near at hand	166

RUSKIN ON EDUCATION

PART FIRST

THE GENERAL PRINCIPLES OF EDUCATION

OF all our contemporaries, since Emerson and Carlyle passed away, there is only one who now fulfils for the nation and for the world the all-important, ever-needed function of the Prophet—John Ruskin. Like the fervid strains of the great Hebrew and Eastern seers, his utterances on a wide range of vital subjects are powerful, eloquent, fearless, enlightened, formative, and pregnant; condemnatory of the present, and hopefully prognostic of the brighter future. Like theirs, too, they are the flashing fires of a burning enthusiasm for God and for humanity; brilliant, self-consuming, and unextinguishable. They demand, and they deserve, attention; and though for a season they are, like all prophetic visions, disregarded by the careless world, they will yet, through their form and character, command and receive recognition. Of their wisdom, there exists, and will long continue to exist, the widest variety of opinion—many, and these a rapidly growing band, holding them as a gospel and a life; more, fearing them as radical and dangerous; most, viewing them as amiable, beautiful, but utopian dreams, impossible of realisation; but all, regarding their author with growing respect, which is rapidly rising to admiration, for his single-eyed sincerity, unsurpassed eloquence, deep love of his fellow-men, and moral insight and elevation.

RUSKIN'S RELATIONS TO EDUCATION

I.—RUSKIN'S VIEWS ON EDUCATION SHOULD BE BETTER KNOWN.

RUSKIN'S opinions on Æsthetic and Social problems have received more exposition and criticism than on other subjects of which he has spoken, numerous and interesting though these have been. Of those less known to the world, on which he has written largely, Education certainly stands first. His views on this all-important theme have received far too little consideration, certainly much less than they deserve, from either critics or students, for the sake alike of their author, their nature, or the subject itself. Light on the vital questions connected with a subject so essential to human happiness and progress, should be welcomed from all quarters, especially when coming from a thinker so original, practical, and advanced, and—doubt it who may—so wise as John Ruskin. It is my own deep and growing sense of the value of his views on Education, and of the comparative neglect they have as yet received—due in part, no doubt, to their being overshadowed by his better-known writings on other subjects—that suggested the desirability of making them matter for general public exposition in these pages, for the instruction of the people. I am more and more convinced, as an educationist, that they form a remarkably enlightened and far-reaching contribution towards the better development of this still very imperfect national and universal function, the training of children, and the education of humanity.

II.—HIS STUDY OF EDUCATION WAS PHILANTHROPIC.

Ruskin's study of Education was the natural outcome of his profound interest in all that bears on the well-being of mankind. His labours in this field have had their root in his philanthropy. In this respect, he resembles Pestalozzi, the greatest educational reformer of modern times, whose enthusiasm in scholastic work sprang from his intense desire to "ennoble men," as he expressed it. He also resembles Froebel, the disciple of the great Swiss, and the founder of the Kindergarten system, which was conspicuously framed for the high moral end of enabling man, in Froebel's own words, "to live a life worthy of his manhood and his species."

The elevated aims of these two remarkable men, who were philanthropists first and educationists second, exactly express those of Ruskin in origin and motive. Feeling like them, and like all others who have desired to raise mankind to higher things—such as philosophers like Plato, religionists like Luther, scientists like Huxley and Spencer—that, to elevate mankind effectively, we must begin at the beginning; to improve the stock, we must operate on the germ; to educate the race, we must train the children.: he was compelled to examine the system by which this training is carried on—in other words, to study Education. Unlike professional educationists, such as Pestalozzi and Froebel, however, Ruskin has not studied Education so fully as he has done some other subjects; he has not examined it as a Science or Art, nor has he formulated any special system, like these technical experts.

His views on teaching are more general and philosophical than technical and scholastic, except on Art, and partly on Literature. At the same time, they are remarkably clear, suggestive, far-reaching, and practical; well-founded on principle, full of dissatisfaction with things as they are, prophetic of desirable reform, and deserving and rewarding careful attention from all interested in educational advancement.

Ruskin's study of Education has, however, been more extensive and thorough than most people would expect, or than even his general readers would think possible, from the time he has given to other matters. For example, the mere index to his educational utterances in *Fors Clavigera* alone fills seven pages; and he tells us (preface to *Deucalion*, 1875), that he proposed writing a life of Xenophon,* for whom he has the highest admiration, which should include an analysis of the general principles of Education, in ten volumes; as well

* Done partly in *Bibliotheca Pastorum*.

as editing "a body of popular literature of entirely serviceable quality—of the most precious books needed," "for a common possession of all our school libraries:"* both of these being gigantic undertakings, which would be a lifework for most men.

III.—HIS OPINION OF EDUCATION AS IT IS.

What is John Ruskin's opinion of Education as it is at present carried on? It is as condemnatory as it is of existing Art and social condition, and as unreservedly and vigorously expressed. "Modern Education," says he, in *Sesame and Lilies*, "for the most part signifies giving people the faculty of thinking wrong on every conceivable subject of importance to them." "Be assured," he asserts, "we cannot read. It is simply and sternly impossible for the English public, at this moment, to understand any thoughtful writing—so incapable of thought has it become in its insanity of avarice;" though, he reassures us, "happily our disease is, as yet, little worse than this

* *Fors Clavigera*, vol. vi., 1876, p. 216.

incapacity of thought." "As a nation," he says, "we have been going on despising literature, despising science, despising art, despising nature, despising compassion, and concentrating our soul on pence." He declares that the development of humanity in England has resulted in "physical ugliness, envy, cowardice, and selfishness," instead of what, "by a conceivably humane, but hitherto unexampled, education, might be attempted of physical beauty, humility, courage, and affection." And he sums up the whole by deliberately declaring this: "The more I see of our national faults or miseries, the more they resolve themselves into conditions of childish illiterateness and want of education in the most ordinary habits of thought. It is, I repeat," he continues, "not vice, not selfishness, not dulness of brain, which we have to lament, but an unreachable schoolboy's recklessness, only differing from the true schoolboy's in its incapacity of being helped, because it acknowledges no master."*

This is a serious indictment, a painful impeachment of a country which plumes itself on its educational eminence among the nations,

* *Sesame and Lilies*, § 40.

and thinks itself, at the worst, second only to Germany in its educational system and results. But Ruskin speaks with deliberation and conviction. " Do you think," asks he, " these are harsh or wild words ? I will prove their truth to you, clause by clause ;"* and he set himself expressly, and, from his point of view, successfully, to make good his accusations, in *Sesame and Lilies*, and elsewhere in his voluminous works, especially in *Fors Clavigera*.

This indictment has been abundantly repeated by Carlyle, Spencer, Huxley, Lyon Playfair, Matthew Arnold and other inspectors of schools, and by many more who are interested in the well-being of the people—in words which it would take too long fully to quote. I give but one example, to show that Ruskin does not stand alone in his low estimate of Education as it exists. Here is the testimony, out of a host, of a fair and unimpassioned judge, Sir John Lubbock,† of what our average school education is; and, in the opinion, he includes all schools, higher and lower :—

"Our great danger in education is, as it seems

* *Sesame and Lilies*, § 31.
† *Addresses Political and Educational*, p. 98.

to me, the worship of book learning—the confusion of instruction and education. We strain the memory, instead of cultivating the mind. The children are wearied by the mechanical act of writing, and the interminable intricacies of spelling; they are oppressed by columns of dates, by lists of kings and places, which convey no definite idea to their minds, and have no near relation to their daily wants and occupations. We ought to follow exactly the opposite course, and endeavour to cultivate their tastes, rather than fill their minds with dry facts.

"Too often, moreover, the acquirement of knowledge is placed before them in a form so irksome and fatiguing that all desire for information is choked, or even crushed out; so that our schools, in fact, become places for the discouragement of learning, and thus produce the very opposite effect from that at which we aim.

"Under the present system, our schools will, I fear, become more and more places of mere instruction; instead of developing intellectual tastes, they will make all mental effort irksome."

IV.—HIS IDEAS OF WHAT EDUCATION SHOULD BE.

Ruskin's central conception of Education, it follows, must surely be something radically and essentially different in type and form from what is generally conceived and carried out in these lands, to give rise to such sweeping condemnation of an educational system, with its mental and moral effects, that has taken so many years and so many hands to build up, and has cost so much in pains and pocket.

It is, down to the ground, as diverse from common conception and practice as it well can be; and it will be good for us, in the remainder of this work, to enquire somewhat into the General Principles which, according to Ruskin and other great educationists, should form the foundation of any true educational system, in theory and practice.

We must, at present, confine ourselves entirely to a few of these general ideas, the subject being in itself so wide; and, even as treated by Ruskin, so broad and so detailed, that it would take volumes even summarily to traverse the ground.

SOME GENERAL PRINCIPLES OF EDUCATION ACCORDING TO RUSKIN

THE TRUE BASIS OF EDUCATION.

I. EDUCATION SHOULD BE REGULATED BY NATURAL ENDOWMENT.—Since Education means, simply and truly, development, the manipulating of existing materials in the human constitution, Ruskin, like all true philosophers, is emphatic on the need of our practical recognition of this fact, and of regulating the treatment of our children according to their constitution and capabilities. These are fixed at birth, being the result of natal and pre-natal conditions, and cannot be changed. "You can't manufacture man," says he, "any more than you can manufacture gold. You can find him, and refine him; you dig him out as he is, nugget-fashion, in the mountain stream; you bring him home, and you make him into current coin, or household plate, but not one grain of him can you originally produce." *

It is, therefore, of the greatest practical moment to discover these capacities in our children, and to utilise and develop them as best we can, varying our treatment and training so as most wisely to secure healthy development, and putting them to the exact work in life they are best fitted for.

The Means of Discovering it.—"You have a certain quantity of a particular sort of intelligence produced for you annually by providential laws, which you can only make use of by setting it to its proper work, and which any attempt to use otherwise involves the dead loss of so much human energy. Well, then, supposing we wish to employ it, how is it to be best discovered and refined? It is easily enough discovered. To wish to employ it is to discover it. All you need is a School of Trial in every important town, in which those idle farmers' lads, whom their masters never can keep out of mischief, and those stupid tailors' 'prentices, who are always putting the

* *A Joy for Ever*, § 20.

sleeves in wrong way upwards, may have a try at this other trade.

"It will be long before the results of experiments now in progress will give data for the solution of the most difficult questions connected with the subject, of which the principal one is the mode in which the chance of advancement in life is to be extended to all, and yet made compatible with contentment in the pursuit of lower avocations by those whose abilities do not qualify them for the higher. But the general principle of Trial Schools lies at the root of the matter—of schools, that is to say, in which the knowledge offered and discipline enforced shall be all a part of a great essay of the human soul, and in which the one shall be increased, the other directed, as the tired heart and brain will best bear, and no otherwise." *

There is no doubt that this suggestion of Ruskin's as to the wisdom and need of having some such testing machinery as he recommends under the name of "Trial Schools," or, as he also calls them, "Searching or Discovering

* *A Joy for Ever*, § 22.

Schools,"* should be more thoroughly and systematically acted upon, than by present blind and imperfect methods is being done. It should receive the practical attention of all educationists and social reformers. As we all feel, and as Ruskin points out again and again, there is a painful waste of mental energy, and loss of existing talent to society, in our haphazard way of ascertaining the precise work in life to which each child should be put, especially the gifted. It is to be feared that it will never be thoroughly done, or be in any way possible, till, as Ruskin points out and recommends, all education shall be truly national, an organic part, and one of the chief functions, of our governing institutions, from the lowest to the highest school, from infant-room to university.

THE OBJECT OF EDUCATION.

II. IT SHOULD NOT BE CONDUCTED WITH A VIEW TO MERE "SUCCESS IN LIFE."— Ruskin holds that our Education is poisoned

* *A Joy for Ever*, § 28.

in its essence, in its root and sap; and that till its central aim is renewed radically and thoroughly, there can never be any true teaching or educational progress. "This arises because it is," he says, "governed and conducted mainly according to the low notion of securing social advancement, which is the gratification of vanity." In his abundant correspondence on Education, he tells us* "he has been always struck by the precedence which the idea of a position in life takes above all other thoughts in the parents'—more especially in the mothers'—minds. The education befitting such and such a *station in life*—this is the phrase, this the object, always. They never seek, as far as I can make out, an education good in itself; even the conception of abstract rightness in training rarely seems reached by the writers. But an education which shall keep a good coat on my son's back—which shall enable him to ring with confidence the visitors' bell at double-belled doors, which shall result ultimately in the establishment of a double-belled door to his own house; in a

* *Sesame and Lilies*, § 2.

word, which shall lead to 'advancement in life.' This we pray for on bent knees, and this is *all* we pray for."

Education should aim at Real Advancement in Living.—These low aims mean, he rightly warns us,* "not indeed to be great in life—'in life itself,' but in its 'trappings;' it means only that we are to get more horses, and more footmen, and more fortune, and more public honour, and—*not* more personal soul."

How true, how sadly true, all this is, we all know; though few, very few of us, dare to say it aloud, still less to denounce it as we ought, and yet less to take practical action to prevent its continuance.

At what, therefore, should Education rightly aim in regard to life? According to Ruskin, at real advancement in life, for which end we must know "what life is." What is real advancement in life? Hear Ruskin's answer: "He only is advancing in life whose heart is getting softer, whose blood warmer, whose brain quicker, whose spirit is entering into Living peace. And the men who have this

* *Sesame and Lilies*, § 42.

life in them are the true lords and kings of the earth—they and they only." *

The only true Education is "an education which, in itself, *is* advancement in life—any other than that may perhaps be advancement in death; and this essential Education might be more easily got or given than we fancy, if we set about it in the right way; while it is for no price and by no favour to be got, if we set about it in the wrong." †

In these fiercely wise words, Ruskin gives eloquent and thrilling utterance to the thoughts of the greatest thinkers of all time. It is the truth sounding ever in dull ears—that "the life is more than meat" or money or ministration to vanity. This is, in another form, Milton's idea of "a complete and generous education;" as "that which fits a man to perform justly, skilfully, and magnanimously, all the duties of all offices." It is another utterance of what Herbert Spencer so well expresses: "How to *live*—that is the essential question for us. The general problem which comprehends every special problem is —the right ruling of conduct in all directions,

* *Sesame and Lilies*, § 42. † *Ibid.* § 2.

under all circumstances. *To prepare us for complete living* is the function which education has to discharge."

That is the true, the only key-note to the harmonies of life. All others, however specious, however common, however honoured, however seductive, are false, "hollow as the grave," and end only in harshest discord.

But alas, alas, Ruskin only utters the sadder and the deeper thoughts of all earnest hearts, when he again says: "I felt, with increasing amazement, the unconquerable apathy in ourselves no less than in the teachers; and that, while the wisdom and rightness of every act and art of life could only be consistent with a right understanding of the ends of life, we were all plunged as in a languid dream—our hearts fat, and our eyes heavy, and our ears closed, lest the inspiration of hand or voice should reach us—lest we should see with our eyes, and understand with our hearts, and be healed."*

"'This intense apathy in all of us, is the first great mystery of life; it stands in the way of every perception, every virtue. There is no making ourselves feel enough astonishment

* *Sesame and Lilies*, § 107.

at it. That the occupations or pastimes of life should have no motive is understandable; but that life itself should have no motive—that we neither care to find out what it may lead to, nor to guard against its being for ever taken away from us—here is a mystery indeed."*

THE FIRST CONDITION OF EDUCATION.

III. EDUCATION SHOULD TRAIN TO USEFUL WORK.—There is nothing that Ruskin considers more essential in all Education than to train the child *to* DO *something*, to make *Work* its central idea. We should provide practical work during the period of school-life, in order to train the child to do practical work in after-life. "Let us, for our lives, do the work of men while we bear the form of them. 'The work of men'—and what is that? Well, we may any of us know very quickly, on the condition of being wholly ready to do it. But many of us are, for the most part, thinking not of what we are to do, but what we are to get." "Whatever our station in life may be," he counsels "those of us who

* *Sesame and Lilies*, § 108.

mean to fulfil our duty ought, first, to live on as little as we can; and, secondly, to do all the wholesome work for it we can, and to spend all we can spare in doing all the sure good we can; and sure good is, first, in feeding people, then in dressing people, and, lastly, in rightly pleasing people, with arts, or sciences, or any other object of thought."*

Therefore, "the *first* condition of Education," he says, "the thing you are all crying out for, is being put to wholesome and useful work. And it is really the *last* condition of it too; you need very little more; but, as things go, there will yet be difficulty in getting that. As things have hitherto gone, the difficulty has been to avoid getting the reverse of that." †

Ruskin's radical conception has been very different from the common one, of making Education a mere knowledge-grinding process, and a means of social advancement and personal aggrandisement.

The most convincing and all-sufficient reason for making Work the end and aim of Education, and the best preparation for life, is, that

* *Sesame and Lilies*, §§ 134-5.
† *Fors Clavigera*, vol. i., 1871, p. 215.

it is the source of all true felicity; it is the secret of happiness in life. " In all other paths by which that happiness is pursued, there is disappointment or destruction; for ambition and for passion, there is no rest, no fruition; the fairest pleasures of youth perish in a darkness greater than their past light; and the loftiest and purest love too often does but inflame the cloud of life with endless fire of pain. But, ascending from lowest to highest, through every scale of human industry, industry worthily followed, gives peace."*

But the work should not be MERE *doing* of *something*, simple action for its own sake, but the doing of something "*useful*," something "*serviceable*." " I believe," says Ruskin, "an immense gain in the bodily health and happiness of the upper classes would follow on their steadily endeavouring, however clumsily, to make the physical exertion they now necessarily exert in amusements, *definitely serviceable*. It would be far better, for instance, that a gentleman should mow his own fields, than ride over other people's." †

* *Sesame and Lilies*, § 128.
† *Frondes Agrestes*, p. 143.

With the vehement indignation of the Baptist to the rich man of his day, Ruskin cries aloud to the rich man of ours: "Build, my man—build or dig—one of the two; and then eat your honestly earned meat, thankfully, and let other people alone, if you can't help them."*

The Kind of Work needed.—Elsewhere he explains, "The three first needs of civilised life are feeding people, dressing people, and lodging people;† and the law for every Christian man and woman is, that they shall be in direct service towards one of these three needs, as far as is consistent with their own special occupation; and if they have no special business, then wholly in one of these services. And out of such exertion in plain duty, all other good will come; for, in this direct contention with material evil, you will find out the real nature of all evil; you will discern, by the various kinds of resistance, what is really the fault and main antagonism to good; also you will find the most unexpected helps and profound lessons given; and truths will come thus down

* *Fors Clavigera*, vol. iv., 1874, p. 259.
† *Sesame and Lilies*, § 135.

to us, which the speculation of all our lives would never have raised us up to. You will find nearly every educational problem solved, as soon as you truly want to do something; everybody will become of use in their own fittest way, and will learn what is the best for them to know in that use. Competitive examination will then, and not till then, be wholesome, because it will be daily, and calm and in practice; and on these familiar arts, and minute, but certain and serviceable knowledges, will be surely edified and sustained the greater arts and splendid theoretical sciences." *

Its Effects on Religion.—" But more than this. On such holy and simple practice will be founded, indeed, at last, an infallible Religion. The greatest of all mysteries of life, and the most terrible, is the corruption of even the sincerest religion, which is not daily founded on rational, effective, humble, and helpful action. Helpful action, observe!

"You may see continually girls who have never been taught to do a single useful thing thoroughly; who cannot sew, who cannot

* *Sesame and Lilies*, § 139.

cook, who cannot cast an account, nor prepare a medicine; whose whole life has been passed either in play or in pride; you will find girls like these, when they are earnest-hearted, cast all their innate passion of religious spirit, which was meant by God to support them through the irksomeness of daily toil, into grievous and vain meditation over the meaning of the great Book, of which no syllable was ever yet to be understood but through a deed; all the instinctive wisdom and mercy of their womanhood made vain, and the glory of their pure consciences warped into fruitless agony concerning questions which the laws of common serviceable life would have either solved for them in an instant, or kept out of their way. Give such a girl any true work that will make her active in the dawn, and weary at night, with the consciousness that her fellow creatures have indeed been the better for her day, and the powerless sorrow of her enthusiasm will transform itself into a majesty of radiant and beneficent peace.

"So with our youths. We once taught them to make Latin verses and called them educated; now we teach them to leap and to row, to hit a ball with a bat, and call them educated. Can they plough, can they sow, can they plant at the right time, or build with a steady hand? Is it the effort of their lives, to be chaste, knightly, faithful, holy in thought, lovely in word and deed?"* *This* it is to be truly educated.

The Relation of Work to Physical Exercise. —So earnest, you see, is this practical philosopher in his advocacy of the work to which our children and our people should be put being definitely "serviceable," that even exercises for physical education should, he holds, not end only in themselves, as in common gymnastics, but should result in something real and practical. He says it is "my steady wish that school boys should learn skill in ploughing and seamanship rather than in cricket; and that young ladies should often be sent to help the cook and housemaid, when they would rather be playing tennis." †

So determined is Ruskin to do what he can to make work, "serviceable labour," an essential part of all education and daily life, and all acquirement "serviceable knowledge," as he

* *Sesame and Lilies*, § 140.
† *Igdrasil*, for August 1890, p. 304.

calls it, that he has made it a condition of entry into St. George's Guild. The candidate has to swear and subscribe his honest hand to this law: "I will labour, with such strength and opportunity as God gives me, for my own daily bread; and all that my hand finds to do, I will do it with my might."

"Any one," he explains in *Fors Clavigera*,* "may be a companion of St. George, who sincerely do what they can to make themselves useful, and earn their own daily bread by their own labour."

We all know that our reformer practises what he preaches, even when, to the outside world, he seems most extreme; and we remember the unwonted enthusiasm he inspired in even the dilletante Oxonians, by leading them for a time to road-making and like serviceable labours, spade and hammer in hand, amid the astonishment and laughter of the British Philistines. He tells us also how he never painted better than after washing down with his hands, on his knees, the wooden stair of a Swiss hotel in which he was staying!

* *Fors Clavigera*, vol. vi., 1876, p. 212.

THE GROWTH OF THIS IDEA IN SCHOOLS.
—This demand of Ruskin for Work as the means and end and test of Education, is daily receiving increased recognition among educationists and social reformers; and it but utters, in new and eloquent and more thorough shape, the aims and ideas of all the best educational philosophers. It is based on the sound principle of all true training of a child, that of developing his faculties by appropriate exercise, which all educational reformers, as far as they have been right, have made the basis of their systems, however varied in form.

It was the central idea in Xenophon's education of Cyrus, whose *Cyropædia* is one of Ruskin's greatest educational books; in Fellenberg's celebrated institution at Hofwyl, in which education was united with and carried on through agriculture; in Robert Owen's Infant schools and philanthropic Communities; in Pestalozzi's educational reforms; in Froebel's Kindergarten system, which is organised, playful work, and in which the intimate union of "hand work and head work" from the first has been lately shown by the issue of a remarkable exposition of the system, in a work under that title by the greatest expounder of Froebel's system, Baroness Bülow.* It has gained increased impulse in the new and growing extension of Manual Instruction, by which pupils are taught to use their hands as well as their heads in school, and not to be ashamed of manual labour; and in its most recent development, through the noteworthy Swedish movement of Otto Salomon, that of Slöyd, whose special object is "the acquirement of manual dexterity, exercise of judgment and technical skill, development of the physique, gradual training of the pupil, by a progressive series of work from simple to skilled workmanship;"† and in the mixed but notable modern cry for Technical Education.

Though Ruskin's idea and advocacy reach further and deeper than these, and signify a more radical change in the matter of labour, throughout society when reconstituted; yet these are encouraging proofs that his notions, however contrary to common practice and traditional opinion, are sound, philosophical,

* *Handwork and Headwork.* (Swan Sonnenschein.)
† *Cyclopædia of Education*, p. 407. (*Ibid.*)

and less utopian than they first seemed. But the dead wall of prejudice and false pride that hides the true dignity of labour from the mass of mankind, both rich and poor, is one still standing broad, high, shameless, and almost unbroken.

Charles G. Leland, the "Hans Breitmann" of the literary world, one of the greatest advocates of practical education that we have, is likewise convinced that it is only "by making *hand work* a part of every child's education that we shall destroy the vulgar prejudice against work as being itself vulgar." He declares that "this prejudice exists where we should least expect to find it—not in the tradition-bound countries of Europe, but in the United States; and that there is no country in the world where manual work is practically in so little respect, or where there are so many trying to get above it, as in the American Republic. While there are a few superior to this rubbishness, there are still millions who are practically enslaved by it." He speaks only simple fact when he further states that "perhaps half the real *suffering* in Europe and America is the result of the effort to appear genteel;" and he names one of the chief causes of this painful pursuit of the false conception of the true gentleman, when he says, that "it arises from the fact that work—hand work—is not yet sufficiently identified with Education and culture."*

Has Ruskin not reason to be angry? Are his burning words too strong in exposing this social sham, and in seeking to lead us to a higher and holier conception, not only of the dignity of labour, but the need, the philosophic wisdom, the redemption for the race, that lies in Work; and in every man, woman, and child on this round earth hourly taking their hard and hearty share in it?

There are signs, though painfully rare and slow, that the world does partially begin to realise, and to act on, Carlyle's words, of which Ruskin's are a perpetual and impassioned commentary: "There is a perennial nobleness, and even sacredness in work. There is always hope in a man that actually and earnestly works; in idleness alone, there is perpetual despair."

* *Practical Education*, by Charles G. Leland. (London, Whittaker & Co., 1888.)

COMPETITIVE EXAMINATIONS.

IV. EDUCATION SHOULD NOT BE ESTIMATED BY THE MERE ACQUISITION OF KNOWLEDGE.—One of the chief tendencies of modern opinion is to estimate Education by means of examinations; and this tendency is one that is yearly growing. This is a natural consequence of the increased desire to make our teaching more thorough, and it is a reaction against the partial and imperfect teaching of the past. But it is attended with many evils —educational, moral, and social; the chief of which is, that it makes mere acquirement, the acquisition of knowledge, the chief end of all education. Instead of this, it is a minor aim, and should be made a means to what is higher —the training of faculty, ability to execute, in the intellectual field, and still better, in the moral world; to give power to live a higher and happier life for one's self and for others. On this subordination of mere knowledge, and the dignifying of the moral elements in Education, Ruskin is most emphatic.

"In the education either of the lower or upper classes," he says, "it matters not the least how much or how little they know, provided they know just what will fit them to do their work and to be happy in it." "A man is not educated," he continues, "in any sense whatsoever, because he can read Latin or write English, or can behave himself in a drawing-room; but he is only educated, if he is happy, busy, beneficent, and effective in the world: millions of peasants are, therefore, at this moment, better educated than most of those who call themselves gentlemen; and the means taken to educate the lower classes in any other sense may very often be productive of a precisely opposite result." *

These are radical but glorious sentiments, that cannot be too much preached in this Philistine age and country, in which mere acquisition, whether of pelf in the pocket or knowledge in the head, is made the test of educational efficiency and rank in society, and not least among the learned classes.

Other enlightened educationists and friends of humanity, believers in true manhood as something different from its market value in the world, have spoken with like vigour and

* *Stones of Venice*, iii., App. vii., p. 232.

indignation against the worship of mere knowledge, which, in our time, is almost as fatal to true character and happiness as the worship of wealth. The matter was expressed pithily by the Lancashire workman to his apprentice, when he said, "Tha wants to know ta mich; tha *do* exactly what a tell tha, and tha'll do reet." *

Never was the rebellion against this tyranny of knowledge in Education better advocated than by Edward Thring, late head-master of Uppingham Public School, an advanced and enlightened educationist of the Ruskin type, who put this and many more of Ruskin's radical positions with epigrammatic point, in spite of his being the chief of an English higher-rank school. He pleaded with teachers to "banish the idolatry of knowledge, to realise that calling out thought and strengthening mind are an entirely different and higher process from the putting in of knowledge and the heaping up of facts." He bade them "choose deliberately a large amount of ignorance, and fling omniscience into the common sewer, if ever they mean to be skilled workmen, masters of

* *Cyclopædia of Education*, p. 202.

mind, lords of thought, and to teach others to be skilled workmen."* "The knowledge-hack and knowledge-omnibus business," he scathingly continues, "may minister to animated steam engines and to intellectual navvies, but it can never teach life or train souls."† "A teacher is not," he says, "a parrot-master, is not a truck-loader at a goods station; but he is one who sows the seeds of life and fosters them."‡

These are sentiments surely expressed quite to Ruskin's heart. They should be made to resound throughout the country, and re-echo in every schoolroom in the land. Happily for teachers, and still more for children, a strong blow to this worship of knowledge and its yard measure of examinations has lately been struck by the virtual abolition of "payment by results" in our Education Codes. It remains to be seen how teachers and examiners will take advantage of the new freedom, by cultivating intelligence more than memory, ability more than acquirement, and character more than all.

* Rawnsley, *Life of Thring*, p. 30.
† *Ibid.* p. 34.   ‡ *Ibid.* pp. 35, 142.

NATURE IN EDUCATION.

V. THE IMPORTANCE OF THE WORLD OF NATURE IN EDUCATION.—Ruskin's name is synonymous with the advocacy of Beauty as an essential element in all culture; he is, beyond question, the greatest apostle of Æsthetic training as necessary for human development and felicity the modern world has yet seen. He holds that "all education to beauty is first"—first in importance and first in time—"in the beauty of gentle human faces round a child; secondly, in the fields." "Without these," he holds, "no one can be educated humanly. He may be made a calculating machine—a walking dictionary—a painter of dead bodies—a twanger or scratcher on keys or catgut—a discoverer of new forms of worms in mud. But a properly so-called human being—never." He advocates, with reiterated, fervid, and poetic eloquence, the importance, the vital need, of training children through intercourse with Nature. Not Wordsworth himself has more than he pleaded for, insisted on, proved, and illustrated the absolute necessity of this open-air element for human training, happiness, health, and progress.

The education of every child should include " heavenly realities ; "—and " see first," he exclaims with ethical and lyrical fervour—" see first that its realities are heavenly, in the fields —in grass, water, beasts, flowers and sky !" Speaking of this training through Nature, he says that there is no part of the subject of Education that he feels more or can press more upon us.* Natural scenes he calls "the pleasant places which God made at once for the schoolroom and the playground of our children ; " † and he declares that "a quiet glade of forest, or the nook of a lake shore, are worth all the schoolrooms in Christendom." ‡

Speaking of the education of girls, after advocating Literature and Art as necessary thereto, he continues : " There is one more help which a girl cannot do without—one which, alone, has sometimes done more than all other influences besides—the help of wild and fair nature." Then he quotes, as an example to be followed

* *Sesame and Lilies*, § 84.
† *Ibid.* § 85.   ‡ *A Joy for Ever*, § 105.

in Britain, De Quincey's account of Joan of Arc's education, in the forests of Domrémy in France; where, De Quincey says, her education was "mean according to the present standard," but "ineffably grand according to a purer philosophic standard,"—a standard Ruskin has never ceased to raise in the eyes of his countrymen.

Crying aloud, as with apocalyptic voice in the existing wilderness of human error in regard to the education of our children, for whom love should impel us to do our best, he says:—

"Oh ye women of England.! from the Princess of Wales to the simplest of you. . . . You cannot baptize your children rightly in those inch-deep fonts of yours, unless you baptize them also in the sweet waters which the great Lawgiver strikes forth for ever from the rocks of your native land—waters which a Pagan would have worshipped in their purity, and you worship only with pollution. You cannot lead your children to these narrow axe-hewn church altars of yours, while the dark azure altars in heaven—the mountains that sustain your island throne—mountains on which a

Pagan would have seen the powers of heaven rest in every wreathed cloud—remain for you without inscription ; altars built, not to but by an Unknown God." *

In this advocacy of Nature, and if possible Wild Nature, of which we have such magnificent and beautiful examples in our own land, easily and cheaply accessible, Ruskin is only emphasising what Pestalozzi and Froebel have already uttered and acted on. I have purposely tried to draw a parallel between this great man, our own master, and these best exponents of modern wise advance in educational science and practice; to show that, even where the outside world are not slow to consider Ruskin extreme and impracticable, his ideas carry with them the seal of the wisest thinkers on the very subjects which the world ignorantly misunderstands and therefore condemns. Speaking of the time that he spent amid the wonderful scenery of Switzerland with Pestalozzi, who made intercourse with Nature in the training of his pupils an integral and regular part of his teaching, Froebel records, in his *Autobiography*, a great and

* *Sesame and Lilies*, § 85.

valuable work, happily now accessible to English readers,* these interesting experiences bearing on the part Nature ought to play in all education :—

"Closely akin to the games in their morally strengthening aspect, were the walks, especially those of the general walking parties, more particularly when conducted by Pestalozzi himself. These walks were by no means always meant to be opportunities for drawing close to Nature; but Nature herself, though unsought, always drew the walkers close to herself. Every contact with her elevates, strengthens, purifies. It is from this cause that Nature, like noble, great-souled men, wins us to her; and whenever school or teaching duties gave me respite, my life at this time was always passed amidst natural scenes and in communion with Nature. From the tops of the high mountains near by, I used to rejoice in the clear and still sunset, in the pine-forests, the glaciers, the mountain meadows, all bathed in rosy light. Such an evening walk came, indeed, to be an almost irresistible necessity to me after each actively

* Translation by Messrs. Charles and Moore, 1886. (Swan, Sonnenschein, & Co.)

spent day. As I wandered on the sunlit, far-stretching hills; or along the still shore of the lake, clear as crystal, smooth as a mirror; or in the shady groves, under the tall forest trees: my spirit grew full with ideas of the truly God-like nature and priceless value of a man's soul, and I gladdened myself with the consideration of mankind as the beloved children of God."

And Froebel has made Nature a necessary part of his system: for as Baroness Bülow, the greatest expounder of Froebel's educational philosophy and practice, says: "Without Nature, the life of the fields and forests, of the animal and vegetable universe, the human being must be without the most essential and natural elements of its development."*

THE OUT-DOOR CLASS-ROOM.

These sentiments, which seem an echo of Wordsworth and Ruskin, are the independent, sober, unimpassioned statement of the practical convictions and conclusions of a philosophic

* *Child and Child Nature*, p. 116.

German, reflecting on the great problems of human development, and its educational process through the daily work of our schoolrooms; and we shall only be wise in our practice when we make them part and parcel of the training of all our children, whether they are immured in our crowded cities or surrounded by natural beauty in the country. It ought to be made an important portion of the weekly work of every school, to take the children out into the country, under the guidance of their several teachers, to breathe its balm, grow strong in its healthy breezes, see and enjoy its beauties, learn to observe accurately and intelligently its varied phenomena, and receive there a glorious training of sense and soul, head and heart, possible only beneath the blue vault of heaven.

All this to be done under as careful guidance and earnest pursuit of intellectual and moral aims as in the schoolroom itself. In truth, the country should—and will, some wiser day— become an outer, uncovered classroom; a Divine museum, utilised by our teachers; the windows of heaven in the sky that illuminate it, opening windows of heaven in the soul, through which the imprisoned spirits of our weary children may gain celestial glimpses of beauty and grandeur, of higher and happier possibilities, and from which our dull and narrow scholastic systems still entirely shut them out.

And this is not Utopia. It has been the blessed experience of many teachers and scholars, and will, some day—God speed it!—become universal; and when that day comes, no compulsory clause will be required in our Codes for that part of the work. It was done in Switzerland; and it is done wherever a true Kindergarten is fully carried out. It has been done by many good schoolmasters, who, rising above scholastic routine, have led their pupils out to the fields, and found there together joys that cannot be uttered.

While I was a teacher myself, I attempted to carry this into practice; and others of my friends have done the same, with unspeakable advantage to themselves and their children. One good teacher in one of the Govan Board Schools, Mr. John Main, an enthusiastic scientist, with broader notions than common of what Education means, has taken his pupils out to Nature for the last fifteen years; and he is still a young man.

Two years ago, his class, the Fourth Standard, made three rambles round Glasgow, and a senior class under him made nine. The numbers ranged from twenty to fifty at a time; and under his guidance, they have visited most places of interest and beauty round the city. In longer journeys, they carry their own provisions, which are washed down with milk from a neighbouring farm, water from the running brook, happy feelings, and healthy appetites.

If this happy practice were at all common—and there is no reason why it should not be universal, except the apathy or ignorance of our teachers—"not a bird should fly unnoticed," as Edward Thring, of Uppingham, who advocated such education, says; "not a song should sound, not a wing be moved, without appealing to seeing eyes and hearing ears." If such were general, "the names of Edward and Robert Dick," he continues, "then would not shine like stars, because of the daylight; and tens of thousands, using happy eyes, would find delight in common things." *

* Rawnsley, *Life of Thring*, p. 18.

OVERPRESSURE.

VI. OUR EDUCATIONAL STANDARD SHOULD NOT BE TOO HIGH.—There are few things on which Ruskin is so persistent and strenuous as in recommending that the faculties of our children ought not to be strained in the education we give them; and that the training and instruction they receive should be specially and intimately adapted to their capacities of mind and body, and to the circumstances in which they live. His counsels in this are peculiarly needed in these days of proved Overpressure and its painful deterioration of individual and national life. There exists a reprehensible ambition, in both parents and teachers, to drive the children beyond their powers, for present paltry gain of fame, or place, or social position, to future certain detriment, and ultimate loss or failure. These are facts that cannot be gainsaid; and it is well that they are receiving more weight and attention from all parties concerned — from physicians, physiologists, educationists, Parliament, and thoughtful persons generally. Ruskin was long as a voice crying in the wilderness on this point, and is still greatly in advance of public opinion in regard to it. Some of his utterances are of the bluntest, but out-and-out wise, and it behoves us as a nation to give them more earnest heed. Among many appeals equally plain and pithy, here is one going straight to the mark; and more need not be said:

"Nor should the natural torpor of wholesome dulness be disturbed by provocations, or plagued by punishments. The wise proverb ought in every schoolmaster's mind to be deeply set—'You cannot make a silk purse of a sow's ear;' expanded with the further scholium that the flap of it will not be the least disguised by giving it a diamond earring. If, in a woman, beauty without discretion be as a jewel of gold in a swine's snout, much more in man, woman or child, knowledge without discretion—the knowledge which a fool receives only to puff up his stomach, and sparkle in his cock's-comb. As I said, in matters moral, most men are not intended to be any better than sheep and robins; so, in matters intellectual, most men are not intended to be wiser than their cocks and bulls,—duly scientific of their yard and pasture, peacefully nescient of all beyond. To be proud and strong, each in his place and work, is permitted and ordained to the simplest; but *ultra—ne sutor, ne fossor.*

"The entire body of teaching throughout the series of *Fors Clavigera* is one steady assertion of the necessity, that educated persons should share their thoughts with the uneducated, and take also a certain part in their labours. But there is not a sentence implying that the education of all should be alike, or that there is to be no distinction of master from servant, or of scholar from clown. That education should be open to all, is as certain as that the sky should be; but, as certainly, it should be enforced on none, and benevolent nature left to lead her children, whether men or beasts, to take or leave at their pleasure. Bring horse and man to the water, and let them drink if, and when, they will: the child who desires education will be bettered by it; the child who dislikes it, only disgraced." *

* *Fors Clavigera*, vol. viii., pp. 257-8-9.

VII. EDUCATION SHOULD VARY WITH CIRCUMSTANCES.—A logical outcome of the position thus maintained by Ruskin is another on which he is equally pungent and pressing— the wisdom and need of adapting the education given to the varying circumstances of the children to be educated. This is radically sound, and is being more and more acted on in Public Schools under the Education Department; but its importance is as yet but dimly perceived, and little practised. The traditions of Popular Education, among both our administrators and teachers, have mostly been against it, and a colourless uniformity has been too much the aim and the result of the methods adopted—a result as far as Nature, against which such a doctrine rebels, has allowed. In combating it, Ruskin waxes more indignant than usual, as in the passage quoted below. This is taken from the invaluable summary of the principles of the Education he has advocated for half a century, given in the concluding volume (vol. viii.) of *Fors Clavigera*, pp. 254–5—a summary that should be read, learnt, and inwardly digested by the nation, and especially by its leaders in both educational and general affairs. Listen to Ruskin :—

"I start with the general principle, that every school is to be fitted for the children in its neighbourhood who are likely to grow up and live in its neighbourhood. The idea of a general education which is to fit everybody to be Emperor of Russia, and provoke a boy, whatever he is, to want to be something better, and wherever he was born, to think it a disgrace to die, is the most entirely and directly diabolical of all the countless stupidities into which the British nation has been of late betrayed by its avarice and irreligion. There are, indeed, certain elements of education which are alike necessary to the inhabitants of every spot of earth. Cleanliness, obedience, the first laws of music, mechanics, and geometry, the primary facts of geography and astronomy, and the outlines of history, should evidently be taught alike to poor and rich, to sailor and shepherd, to labourer and shop-boy. But for the rest, the efficiency of any school will be found to increase exactly in the ratio of its direct adaptation to the circumstances of the children it receives; and the quantity of knowledge to be attained in a given time being equal, its value will depend on the possibilities of its instant application. You need not teach botany to the sons of fishermen, architecture to shepherds, or painting to colliers; still less the elegances of grammar to children, who, throughout the probable course of their total lives, will have, or ought to have, little to say, and nothing to write."

THE THREE R'S.

VIII. THE PREVALENT ESTIMATE OF THEIR VALUE IS ERRONEOUS.—On no subject, not even excluding his views on Interest in money matters, are Ruskin's ideas on Education more antagonistic to prevalent traditional opinion and general practice than those on "the three R's," Reading, Writing, and Arithmetic. In one word, if certain elements which are higher and better are not taught and trained in our schools, he would not have these subjects, which had so long been reckoned essentials, taught at all! On this matter, he uses no dubiety of speech or practice whatever; he speaks quite straight.

He says, "I do not choose to teach," in his own schools of St. George, "(as usually understood), the three R's; first, because, as I *do* choose to teach the elements of music, astronomy, botany, and zoology, not only the masters and mistresses capable of teaching these should not waste their time on the three R's; but the children themselves would have no time to spare, nor should they have." He would have these taught at home by their parents, or by the children to each other.

He goes on to say: "Secondly, I do not care that St. George's children, as a rule, should learn either reading or writing, because there are very few people in this world who get any good by either. Broadly and practically, whatever foolish people *read* does *them* harm; and whatever they *write* does other people harm; and nothing can ever prevent this, for a fool attracts folly as decayed meat attracts flies, and distils and assimilates it, no matter out of what book."

He tells how he "wrote privately, with some indignation, to the Companion of St. George who had ventured to promise to teach them."

Her reply that "Inspectors of Schools now required the three R's imperatively," evoked the remonstrance "with indignation at high pressure, that ten millions of Inspectors of Schools collected on Cader Idris should not make him teach in his schools, come to them who liked, a single thing he did not choose to!"*

These, at first sight, seem not only extraordinary sentiments, but they appear to outrage common-sense, in regard to subjects that are thought to be the necessary instruments for all education, as generally understood. But Ruskin knows well where he stands in this, as in other subjects on which he runs counter to received opinion, and can give the fullest reasons for the faith that is in him.

What, then, are the grounds of his astonishing position in this matter?

The gist of them may be stated in one sentence: It is far better that the three R's should not be taught to our children, if certain other subjects which are infinitely more important are omitted.

What are these more important subjects in

* *Fors Clavigera*, vol. viii., p. 232.

Ruskin's eyes? They are these, as briefly summarised by himself:—

"Every parish school should have a garden, playground, and cultivable land round it, or belonging to it, spacious enough to employ the scholars in fine weather, mostly out of doors.

"Attached to the building, a children's library, in which the scholars who *care* to read may learn that art as deftly as they like, by themselves, helping each other without troubling the master. A sufficient laboratory always, in which shall be specimens of all common elements of natural substances, and where simple chemical, optical, and pneumatic experiments may be shown; and, according to the size and importance of the school, attached workshops, many or few,—but always a carpenter's, and, first of those added in the better schools, a potter's."[*]

Shortly stated, Ruskin holds that certain practical, intellectual, and moral elements— those of the hand, head, and heart—are inexpressibly more important to personal and national happiness and well-being than any

[*] *Fors Clavigera*, vol. viii., p. 239.

amount of dexterity in the three R's. These should therefore be taught and trained, whether the so-called essentials are taught or not; and where these higher, more vital elements are neglected, it would be better that the lesser should be omitted. He gives full reasons for these positions, which would detain us here too long. He does not, mark you, object to the three R's in themselves, but seeks to put them into the inferior place they ought to occupy as compared with other subjects which have hitherto been generally neglected.

In teaching the three R's, when they are taught, Ruskin would also have much less time devoted to them; and he advocates certain reforms in their treatment in our schools. Arithmetic, in particular, he would give comparatively little attention to—certainly not a tithe of what is now given to it—truly considering that our children are kept at this subject as if they were all to become shopkeepers. Among other scholastic technicalities with which young people are annoyed, he inveighs strongly against Grammar as generally treated, saying that he is "at total issue with most preceptors as to the use of grammar to *anybody.*" The whole of his observations on these portions of our common school curriculum are unusually wise and suggestive, and they deserve the earnest attention of all teachers, and makers of Codes and text-books for the guidance of teachers, however diverse his views are from general doctrine and practice.

His central attitude on the relation between the three R's and the higher matters which he would make the staple work of our schools in their place, is thus finely put by him in his *Crown of Wild Olive* (§ 144), in words that should be graven on the hearts of all our teachers, and printed in golden capitals at the head of all our Codes :—

"Education does not mean teaching people to know what they do not know—it means teaching them to behave as they do not behave. It is not teaching the youth of England the shapes of letters and the tricks of numbers, and then leaving them to turn their arithmetic to roguery and their literature to lust. It is, on the contrary, training them into the perfect exercise and kingly continence of their bodies and souls, by kindness, by watching, by warning, by precept, and by praise—but, above all, by example."

It is well—nay, all important—that we should hear such vigorous and well-grounded protests against our prevalent idolatry of the mere instruments of knowledge, which have too long usurped the place of the truly essential elements of education, as here stated by this master of English, and pioneer of educational reform.

His condemnation of the three R's may indeed be too sweeping; but it is rightly founded on principle; and the excess in his recommendations is due mainly to his righteous indignation at the time of so many generations of children being wasted over their excessive acquisition, and at the exclusion of more vital elements in the true culture of our people.

It is not the first time that like vigorous protest has been entered against this slavery to traditional opinion. A good many years ago, the late Professor Hodgson, of Edinburgh, for example, published an appeal against *The Over-estimate of the Three R's* in our common school work; and other criticisms in the same direction, almost as pungent as Ruskin's, might be quoted, but these would take us too far.

What a remarkable and generally unknown commentary all this is on the history of our National Education, as conducted and subsidised by Parliamentary enactment, in the English Education Code of 1870, and the Scotch of 1872! In these, the three R's, thus despised and relegated to a very subordinate place as educational elements by Ruskin and others, were made the total of the education sanctioned and paid for in our elementary State-aided schools; as the only ones needed and allowed, by our wise rulers and Code makers, for the children of the land, who were to become the future citizens of the country, and the parents of the generations to come; and as the only means by which they were prepared for the momentous functions of personal, domestic, and political life, on which the welfare and progress of the nation are founded.

The subjects Ruskin recommends as the basis and staple of the training he would displace these over-estimated elementary instruments by, he explains in full detail in various places; but these matters are beside our purpose here, which is simply to expound the general principles advocated by this great master of Educational and Social Science.

THE IMPORTANCE OF RUSKIN'S VIEWS.

But, however beautiful and attractive these refreshing and unconventional opinions of our eloquent and pungent critic of Education are, space prevents further enlargement. As already remarked, Ruskin's utterances on the subject cover the most of the field, and his observations are not only comprehensive, but, for a philosophical, non-professional observer, remarkably detailed. It would be well for the country to know more of this great thinker's views and suggestions on these all-important and ever-pressing themes; so wise, so fresh, so needed, and so securely vitalising do I consider his ideas, so well calculated to rouse us from a false ideal, and point the way to higher and happier and healthier things, in what we are all vitally interested, the educating and training of our children. Indeed, had I time,

I should try to do for Ruskin what I did fifteen years ago for George Combe,*—that is, present, in systematic form, his scattered observations on educational principles and practice; and for the same reason, in the case of both of these otherwise dissimilar men, who, in the matter of Education, are wisely and happily in unison—viz., the light their conceptions are calculated to throw on the difficult problems involved, and the wise guidance they are able to give in moulding future teaching. Whoever will devote himself to what some day will no doubt be done—to the great but delightful task of gathering, collating, and classifying Ruskin's utterances on Education—will not only do honour to himself and his master, but provide, for general and accessible use, a work of highest value, to regulate and elevate the Education of the future.

It is well for us, it would be well for the world, and it would be wise for those who have the administration of educational affairs, in all countries, to realise the central conception that runs through all Ruskin's utterances

* In *Education, its Principles and Practice as developed by George Combe.* (Macmillan & Co., 1879.)

on Education, whether of criticism or suggestion, by virtue of which they differ so widely from the common practice of the day. This conception is, that the chief aim and end of all human teaching, in home and school, should be ethical—a training not primarily for the possession of any accomplishments or for social success, but for the performance of Duty, for doing, in the healthiest, happiest, and completest way, the daily work of life. Herein lies its specialty: it is this that constitutes it a needed Gospel in Education; a message required never more than now, in these money-worshipping, position-loving, property-pursuing, yet momentous and hopeful times.

We require, as a people, to realise that "Education, briefly," as Ruskin once more summarises it, "is the leading human souls to what is best, and making what is best out of them; and that these two objects are always attainable together, and by the same means; that the training which makes men *happiest in themselves* also makes them *most serviceable to others.*" *

* *Stones of Venice*, iii., App. vii. (p. 226 of the 1887 edition). The whole passage is very fine.

OUR EXISTING EDUCATIONAL IDEAL LOW AND DEFECTIVE.

Mere knowledge, acquirements, accomplishments, however great or brilliant, are as dust to diamonds compared with this. Yet our schools are esteemed, organised, and regulated mostly on opposite notions.

So consistent, so earnest and thoroughgoing, however, is Ruskin, that he repeatedly and unreservedly declares that he "would never wish to see a child taught to read at all, unless the other conditions of its education were alike gentle and judicious;"* so deadly and so venomous, he holds, is mere knowledge, encyclopædic though it be, that is not regulated by higher principle. And who among us would dare to say otherwise? Yet, though we profess to agree with him in words, as a people, we deny it in deeds; we have never made provision in our codes and time-tables for systematic teaching and training in morals, as we have done for other and less important matters.

As Edward Thring once more indignantly

* *Best* 100 *Books*, p. 8.

and rightly declares,—"In England, we are cutting our children in half; we are, in our systems of education, so leaving out of count that love, and truth, and temperance, and joy, and sorrow, and love of God, and endurance of pain are things teachable, that we are, in our search for intellect, allowing national character to suffer loss in the training."* "The idolatry of knowledge must perish," he continues, in prophetic strain, "or education cannot begin. Noble character, this is what our teachers must strive for in their pupils." †

We require to change our ideal of Education. In all our straining after better teaching, in all improvements in our Education Codes, we shall never succeed in our aim, however much we do, however much we spend, unless we make the higher elements in it foremost and all pervading; unless we act on the true type of the educated man, sketched by Ruskin, as one who "has understanding of his own uses and duties in the world, and who has so trained himself, or been so trained, as to turn, to the best and most courteous account,

* Rawnsley, *Life of Thring*, p. 26.
† *Ibid.* p. 27.

whatever faculties or knowledge he has;" and unless, amid our over-grown luxury and selfish refinement, we also perceive, and act on the perception, that the ideal of human education, as of human life, is "a union of Spartan simplicity of manners with Athenian sensibility and imagination."*

* *A Joy for Ever*, Addenda, § 147.

PART SECOND

THE TRAINING OF TASTE IN SCHOOLS

OF neglected elements in our Education, there has none been more forgotten than the Æsthetic. We have improved in many points in our recent educational advances, but have, till but yesterday, totally overlooked the training of Taste in our children, as an important and necessary part of a full course of human development. We are, as a people, creditably intellectual, fairly moral, earnestly if not superstitiously religious, and eminently and prosaically practical; but æsthetic or refined, little or not at all. And what is worse, we pride ourselves on its want, deeming devotion to things of taste weakness, and proving the point by calling it French polish or Italian dilettantism.

This is matter for the deepest regret; it is a national loss, in character and happiness, that should command the earnest attention of all interested in national progress. There are growing signs of improvement in this respect, but as yet only among the few; and some of these have advocated the subject in a way that has tickled popular humour, roused ridicule, and caused revolt instead of advance in this despised but vital direction—a grave neglect being hidden and perpetuated by confounding the weak extravagances of sun-flower æsthetes with true culture, and by ignorantly reckoning instruction in Art as a means only for promoting, as Ruskin says, "habits of mind which, in their more modern developments in Europe, have certainly not been advantageous to nations or indicative of worthiness in them."*

* *A Joy for Ever.* Supplementary papers, "Education in Art," § 154.

THE NEED FOR CULTIVATING TASTE IN SCHOOLS

I.—THE NATURE OF TASTE.

IN this work, the word Taste is used as a short and convenient synonym for æsthetic pleasure—delight in the Beautiful in all its forms.

Taste it is difficult or impossible scientifically to define — at least, to give it complete and exhaustive expression. It is piquantly and practically put by Ruskin in words sufficient for all useful purposes, as "the instantaneous preference of the noble thing to the ignoble:"* a phrase which embodies its central idea and aim. This conception has been expanded into an endless variety of formulæ. It has been designated "sympathetic admiration of

* *A Joy for Ever.* Supplementary papers, "Education in Art," § 154.

the Beautiful and Sublime;" by Véron, as "a lively natural sensibility to the impressions of the eye and ear;" and as "delight in the Ideal."

It is not our purpose now to analyse this feeling, more or less possessed by all human beings, but to consider the best means of cultivating this love for the Beautiful.

THE CHIEF GROUPS OF THE ÆSTHETIC ARTS.

This delightful emotion manifests itself in two chief directions, according to its medium of expression through the eye and through the ear. These two representative organs divide Æsthetics and the Arts they create into two main groups:—

THE ARTS OF THE EYE: Painting, Sculpture, Architecture.

THE ARTS OF THE EAR: Music, Dancing, Poetry.

Here we shall chiefly, if not wholly, confine ourselves in this extensive field to the arts of the eye, those of Painting (in which is included Drawing), Sculpture, and Architecture.

HOW MUCH MAY BE ESSAYED IN THE CULTIVATION OF TASTE.

It will be our endeavour to inquire how the general culture of our people can best be achieved through the feeling for the Beautiful as perceived by the eye, under the conviction, as expressed by Ruskin, that true taste is "a necessary accompaniment of high worthiness in nations or men." * In considering this, it is well not to expect too much, but at once to see and acknowledge, with Ruskin, that "it is not to be acquired by seeking it as our chief object, since the first question, alike for man and for multitude, is not at all what they are to like, but what they are to do; and fortunately so, since true taste, so far as it depends on original instinct, is not equally communicable to all men; and, so far as it depends on extended comparison, is unattainable by men employed in narrow fields of life. We shall not succeed," he continues, "in making a peasant's opinion good evidence on the merits of the Elgin and Lycian marbles; nor is it

* *A Joy for Ever.* Supplementary papers, "Education in Art," § 154.

TRAINING OF TASTE IN SCHOOLS 69

necessary to dictate to him in his garden the preference of gilly-flower or of rose ; yet we may make Art a means of giving him helpful and happy pleasure, and of gaining for him "— what Ruskin ever rightly insists on as the end of all true education, public or private, scholastic or personal—"serviceable knowledge ; "* as we found in early chapters in this series.

THE VITAL IMPORTANCE OF CHILDHOOD IN ITS TRAINING.

If we are to train the individual and the nation to derive pleasure from what is beautiful or artistic, it would at once seem to be evident that we should take steps to create this pleasure, this finer perception, at the most susceptible period of life, before the child's taste has been blunted or vitiated by the sight of the ugly and degraded. This period is, of course, that of childhood and youth, the time of his general education, when his whole being, under a wise system of training, should be subjected systematically to a harmonious

* *A Joy for Ever.* "Education in Art," § 154.

development of its varied faculties, so as to produce an educated man, one who is, as Ruskin wisely describes him, "happy, busy, beneficent and effective in the world;" the true aim of all education being again, according to him, "the leading of human souls to what is best, and making what is best out of them." * If it is an all-important first duty of a state to see that every child born therein shall be educated in the traditional elements of instruction, in "the three R's" of all knowledge, and like accepted subjects; it is equally its duty to see that every child shall be trained to have an "instantaneous preference of the noble thing to the ignoble," to have a love for the Beautiful and the Good.

Surely, while the child's susceptibilities are most plastic, while he is receiving impressions for good or evil that are indelible and life-long, it would be our wisdom, as it certainly is our duty, to surround him with what is lovely, to saturate his eye and ear and soul with the Beautiful, so that his pleasure in it becomes, as far as possible, instantaneous and delightful, so that he will turn with pain, if not

* *Stones of Venice*, iii., App. vii.

loathing, from all that is ugly and degrading. In undertaking this part of his education, we ought firmly to believe with Ruskin that "in the make and nature of every man, however rude or simple, there are some powers for better things; some tardy imagination, torpid capacity of emotion, tottering steps of thought, there are, even at the worst; and in most cases, it is all our own fault that they *are* tardy and torpid. But they cannot be strengthened unless we are content to take them in their feebleness, and unless we prize and honour them in their imperfection above the best and most perfect manual skill."

If we were wise, we should also act on the conviction, however utopian or extravagant it may appear to many men, as uttered by the same authority, that "all education to beauty is first—in the beauty of gentle human faces round a child; secondly, in the fields—fields meaning grass, water, beasts, flowers, and sky. Without these, no man can be educated humanly."

"The whole period of youth is one essentially of formation, edification, instruction. I use these words with their weight in them; intaking of stores, establishment in vital habits, hopes, faiths. There is not an hour of it but is trembling with destinies, not a moment of which, once passed, the appointed work can ever be done again, or the neglected blow struck on the cold iron. Take your vase of Venice glass out of the furnace and strew chaff over it in its transparent heat, and recover *that* to its clearness and rubied glory when the north wind has blown upon it; but do not think to strew chaff over the child fresh from God's presence and to bring the heavenly colours back to *him*, at least in this world."

THE IMPORTANCE OF THE SCHOOL-ROOM FOR THIS TRAINING.

But the homes of the mass of our children, especially in our great cities, are too often sordid and unlovely, and not seldom vile. Their parents are, as a whole, ignorant or careless; and even with all their affection for their offspring, which is as genuine and as deep as in more favoured circles, they are unable to provide the means of training to beauty or culture of any kind. It therefore becomes a national duty to supply the training thus lacking to these children in their homes, and in the stony streets, by seeing that it is furnished elsewhere, under the best conditions—in the schoolrooms into which we gather them for their education. It is there only that the training of the intellectual and moral faculties of most of our children can be carried on; and on account of the mean surroundings of their dwellings, it is there alone that we can achieve in any degree the training of their æsthetic faculties, their gradual perception and love of the Beautiful. Hence the importance of our schools in this branch of culture, for there alone exist the means of higher culture to them.

Ruskin, perceiving this, would surround all our little ones with beauty in their schools, which, he truly says, are "the first and most important kind of public buildings" into which we ought to "introduce some great changes in the way of decoration." He laments the general state of our schoolrooms as they have been in the past.

OUR SCHOOLS DEVOID OF TASTE IN THE PAST.

"Hitherto," he says,* "it has either been so difficult to give all the education we wanted to our children, that we have been obliged to do it, if at all, with cheap furniture and bare walls; or else we have considered that cheap furniture and bare walls are a proper part of the means of education; and supposed that boys learned best when they sat on hard forms, and had nothing but blank plaster about and above them whereupon to employ their spare attention; also, that it was as well they should be accustomed to rough and ugly conditions of things, partly by way of preparing them for the hardships of life, and partly that there might be the least possible damage done to floors and forms, in the event of their becoming, during the master's absence, the fields or instruments of battle.

"I believe," he continues, "the notion of fixing the attention by keeping the room empty is a wholly mistaken one. I think it is just in the emptiest room that the mind wanders

* *A Joy for Ever*, § 104.

most; for it gets restless, like a bird, for want of a perch, and casts about for any possible means of getting out and away.

"And even if it be fixed by an effort on the business in hand, that business becomes itself repulsive, more than it need be, by the vileness of its associations; and many a study appears dull or painful to a boy when it is pursued on a blotted deal desk, under a wall with nothing on it but scratches and pegs, which would have been pursued pleasantly enough in a curtained corner of his father's library, or at the lattice window of his cottage. Nay, my own belief is, that the best study of all is the most beautiful." *

THE TWO WAYS OF TRAINING TASTE IN SCHOOL.

This training of the Taste of our children in school may be carried on in two ways— passively and actively—by the *passive* and *insensible* influence of the scholars' surroundings in the school; and by the *active* and *determinate* education of their Taste, through

* *A Joy for Ever*, § 105.

various means undertaken by the teacher for that end. Here we shall be obliged to confine ourselves almost entirely to the *insensible training of taste in and by our schools*.

SCHOOLS SHOULD BE REFINED IN ARCHITECTURE AND DECORATION.

For this purpose, Ruskin would surround the whole school-life of our children with beautiful things. Our schools should all be, according to him, of "refined architectural decoration," nay, they should be "noble" and "castellated"; and he looks forward to the day, after we become wiser, happier, and better educated, when such "noble groups" will arise all over England. This much for their external appearance.

Their interior he would have artistically adorned; and for the decoration of the walls of the class-rooms, he specially recommends "historical painting." He complains, and rightly, that "we have hitherto been in the habit of conveying all our historical knowledge, such as it is, by the ear only, never by the eye; all our notions of things being ostensibly derived from verbal description, not from sight." He has "no doubt, that as we gradually grow wiser, we shall discover at last that the eye is a nobler organ than the ear; and that through the eye we must, in reality, obtain, or put into form, nearly all the useful information we have about this world." *

"The use of decorative paintings on the school walls would be, in myriads of ways, to animate their history for them, and to put the living aspect of past things before their eyes as faithfully as intelligent invention can; so that the master shall have nothing to do but once to point to the schoolroom walls, and for ever afterwards, the meaning of any word would be fixed in a boy's mind in the best possible way. Is it a question of classical dress—what a tunic was like, or a chlamys, or a peplus? At this day, you have to point to some vile wood-cut in the middle of a dictionary page, representing the thing hung upon a stick; but then, you would point to a hundred figures, wearing the actual dress, in its fiery colours, in all actions of various stateliness or strength; you would understand

* *A Joy for Ever*, § 106.

at once how it fell round the people's limbs as they stood, how it drifted from their shoulders as they went, how it veiled their faces as they wept, how it covered their heads in the day of battle." *

THE VIEWS OF ANCIENT THINKERS.

In all this, extravagant and costly as it may seem to some, Ruskin is but expressing, in his own inimitable way, the thoughts of some of the best thinkers in all time, regarding the higher culture of our children—from the long departed ages of the wise and cultured Egyptians, whose temples and cities by the Nile were a series of picture-galleries, down to the present day, when our blind eyes are gradually opening to the importance of this neglected part of education. We are now only beginning—and very slowly beginning—to realise this in the nineteenth century after Christ, five thousand years after the Egyptians saw and acted on it; what the Greeks realised and acted on four centuries before Christ, especially in the age of Perikles.

* *A Joy for Ever*, § 107.

"We ought," says Plato, "to seek out artists who, by the power of genius, can trace out the nature of the fair and graceful, that our young men, dwelling, as it were, in a healthful region, may drink in good from every quarter whence any emanation from noble works may strike upon their eye or their ear, like a gale wafting health from salubrious lands; and win them imperceptibly from their earliest years into resemblance, love, and harmony with the true beauty of reason. Because he that has been duly nurtured therein will have the keenest eye for defects, whether in the failures of art, or in the misgrowths of nature; and feeling a most just disdain for them, will commend beautiful objects, and gladly receive them into his soul, and *feed* upon them, and grow to be noble and good; whereas he will rightly censure and hate all repulsive objects, *even in his childhood, before he is able to be reasoned with;* and when reason comes, *he* will welcome her most cordially who can recognise her by the instinct of relationship, and because he has been thus nurtured." *

* Compayre's *History of Pedagogy.*

ÆSTHETIC EDUCATION IN ATHENS.

And this was greatly—nay, wonderfully—a reality in the life and training of Athenian youth.

"The Athenian of the age of Perikles," says Augustus Wilkins, in his admirable little work on *National Education in Greece*, "was living in an atmosphere of unequalled genius and culture. He took his way past the temples, where the friezes of Phidias seemed to breathe and struggle, under the shadow of the colonnades reared by the craft of Iktinus or Kalikrates, and glowing with the hues of Polygnotus, to the agora, the forum, the marketplace, where, like his Aryan forefathers by the shores of the Caspian, or his Teutonic cousins in the forests of Germany, he was to take his part as a free man in fixing the fortunes of his country."

"What could books do more for a man who was receiving an education such as this? It was what the student gazed on, what he heard, what he caught by the magic of sympathy, not what he read, which was the education furnished by Athens. Not by her discipline, like Sparta and Rome, but by the unfailing charm of her gracious influence did Athens train *her* children."

THE VIEWS OF MONTAIGNE AND FENELON.

"Were it left to my ordering," exclaims Montaigne, after indignantly and as wrathfully as it was possible for his gentleness, condemning the severities of the school-life of his time, "were it left to my ordering, I should paint the school with the pictures of Joy and Gladness, Flora and the Graces, as the philosopher Speusippus did his school, that where their profit is, they might there have pleasure too. Such viands as are proper and wholesome for children," he continues in figure, "should be seasoned with sugar, and such as are dangerous to them, with gall." *

Fenelon also expresses delightfully true and advanced thoughts in regard to the importance of the element of the Beautiful and the attractive in early education. He condemns the wearisome and gloomy class-rooms of his

* *Essays*, Book I., chap. 25.

time, in 1680, when he was thirty years of age, where the teachers were ever talking to children of words and things of which they understood nothing. "There was no liberty, no enjoyment, but always lessons, silence, uncomfortable postures, correction, and threats."

In the education of his time, and it is too true of our own, "all the pleasure was put on one side, and all that was disagreeable on the other; the disagreeable was all put into the study, and all the pleasure was found in the diversions." For study, as for moral discipline, according to Fenelon, pleasure must do all.

"Into a reservoir so little and so precious as a child's mind, only exquisite things should be poured," as he finely expresses it. In his endeavour to avoid the repulsive in education, however, he is apt, perhaps, to go too far in his righteous rebellion against the evil methods of his time; as, when he asks that the books of the pupils shall be "beautifully bound with gilt edges and fine pictures;"* and yet we have abundantly realised this last, in exquisite

* Compayre's *History of Pedagogy*, pp. 170-3.

illustrations in the everyday reading-books of our own time!. We have only to go further, and recognise Æsthetic Culture as equally binding on us in other directions in the training of our children.

OTHER OPINIONS COINCIDENT.

Time would fail us to cite other advocacy of this training, such as the wise rhetoric of the great educational innovator, Rousseau; the eloquent pleadings of Richter; the philosophic educational utterances of Froebel, in whose Kindergarten system Æsthetic development, by active and passive training, forms a prominent, attractive, and most effective feature from the first—being indeed the most detailed and best graduated Æsthetic course for schools yet devised.

I would only conclude the citation of these eminent authorities in favour of this neglected element in our education, by referring to the opinion of two thinkers of our own day.

That dry, hard-headed philosopher, John Stuart Mill, in his rectorial address at St. Andrews, urged Æsthetic training as " needful to the completeness of the human being," and as "deserving to be regarded in a more serious light than is the custom of these countries."

John Stuart Blackie, whose educational labours deserve more recognition than they have received, says in one of his most recent volumes: "Specially, let the schoolmaster take a leaf from the wisdom of the ancient Egyptians, who learned much from picture-writing long before letters were invented or books were in general circulation. Let him take care that the walls of the schoolroom be hung round with speaking portraits of all the great and good heroes and heroines of national and general history, as also with striking presentations of the picturesque scenes, famous cities, and historic sites, that mark the dramatic movements of human progress; for these will remain through life, and compass their bearer with a rich array of monitory witnesses, long after whole volumes of dim record and long columns of unfructifying dates shall have passed into oblivion." *

* On "The Philosophy of Education," in *Essays on Social Subjects*, 1890.

II.—WHAT HAS BEEN DONE TOWARDS THE REALISATION OF THESE PRINCIPLES?

In view of these philosophical principles of the science of Education, by which Æsthetic training is proved to be a necessary and important element in the full development of humanity, thus expounded and recommended by the more enlightened thinkers, it becomes an interesting and natural inquiry—What has been done to carry these principles into practice in our schools? The simple answer is that, until recently, little or nothing has been attempted in this direction. This neglect is due in largest measure to the general backward condition of Education up till the present century, and the want of sufficient enlightenment on the subject among those concerned with the conduct of Education; and also, as suggested already by Ruskin, to the difficulty of securing even the bare elements of the three R's in *Common* schools, and the devotion to certain traditional subjects, notably the dead languages, in our *Higher Grade* schools.

THE BEGINNING OF AN ÆSTHETIC REVIVAL.

Indeed, in Britain, it was not till the passing of the English Education Act of 1870, and the Scotch Act of 1872, that our educational authorities took any steps to provide for the training of Taste in Common Schools, by means of architecture, furnishing, or otherwise. At that time, the new public interest roused in National Education, and the enlightened policy of some of the more prominent School Boards, created what may be justly characterised as a new era, not only in general school provision and work, but markedly in improved æsthetic conditions, in the premises erected for the education of the mass of the people—an advance far ahead of what has yet been done in the Higher Schools for the wealthy. School Boards in general, and some Boards in particular, provided and furnished buildings architecturally palatial as compared with their predecessors, and internally, well furnished and sometimes tastefully adorned. The Boards of most of the larger cities have shown praiseworthy examples in this particular. At the same time, it cannot be said that anywhere has the importance of Æsthetic Education, by passive adornment and active training, been sufficiently recognised as a determinate and practical part of the daily work of our schools.

III.—THE MEANS OF ÆSTHETIC CULTIVATION IN SCHOOLS.

To come to the practical side of the subject: How are the managers and teachers in our Common Schools to provide for the Æsthetic Education of our children? There is no lack of means of a good kind, provided there exists the desire—the way is easy if the will is there. Happily, every year witnesses an increase of beautiful materials at surprisingly low prices.

1. SCHOLASTIC DIAGRAMS.—The maps, diagrams of a wide variety, representations of the animal and vegetable world, pictures of scenery, cabinets of objects, are abundant and good, and easily within the reach of all who

wish for them; and many schools are well supplied with these. I should deprecate, in this connection, the exhibition, on the walls, of physiological charts, with sections of the human frame and its organs, which, however useful for teaching purposes, are unpleasant, often painfully ugly, and certainly not conducive to taste or refined feeling. These yet disfigure the walls of many schools, neither managers nor teachers seemingly noticing their incongruity and offence; this very blindness being an additional proof that we have not awakened to the means and aims of education on its Æsthetic side.

2. SPECIAL ÆSTHETIC DECORATIONS.—But for the cultivation of Taste in schools, much more is required than the exhibition of such objects and diagrams, which, however pleasing in colour and arrangement, are primarily educational, and not artistic, in their aim. We ought to provide other things *directly intended for Æsthetic purposes*, for the cultivation of the feeling for the Beautiful—in good drawings, engravings, photographs, pictures, both plain and coloured; portraits of the great

and good of the earth; historical scenes by eminent artists; busts of all kinds, of which an ever-increasing variety is being cheaply provided, including the best of classical antiquity and of modern art; architectural designs, and photos of the most beautiful buildings in the world, many of which are now produced large, beautiful, and effective; and, among other good reproductions, some of the pretty coloured pictures from the Christmas numbers of the illustrated journals, especially those of beautiful children, the very sight of which it is a pleasure to see in our schools, where they often appear. In all these lines, materials are abundant and good, and yearly increase in number and improve in character, both with and without colour. Several societies exist for the purpose of providing artistic materials for school decoration, the yearly issues of which should be better known and more utilised by school managers and friends of Education generally.*

* Two of these may be mentioned: "The Art for Schools Association," 29 Queen Square, Bloomsbury, London, from which catalogues of their beautiful reproductions can be had; and "The Fitzroy Picture Society," 20 Fitzroy Street, London, W.

3. ILLUSTRATIONS IN SCHOOL BOOKS. — In this connection, there is one medium by which much may be done for the cultivation of the taste of the individual pupils—that of artistic illustration of school books, especially for the teaching of reading, geography, and history. In no department of educational furnishings has such marked advance been made as here, especially in Reading books and Geographical Readers, many of which are brightened with beautiful engravings; especially by firms, like Blackie and Nelson, which utilise for school purposes the exquisite engravings they produce for artistic books of a costly kind—many of them being simply charming. This is a field that should be specially cultivated by all interested in Education, including publishers. It is one that might effect an improvement in Taste above even wall decoration, as these beautiful presentations are ever before the pupils' eyes, both at home and in school, and might, and no doubt do, influence the parents as well as the children. Much more should be done, however, by teachers, to increase the effect of these illustrations, and cultivate the taste of the young through their means; by

directing their attention to their beauty, and pointing out to, and, still better, drawing from, their scholars the artistic elements in these fine engravings, the use of which is yearly becoming more common for educational purposes.

4. PLANTS AND FLOWERS. — Another and delightful means of æsthetic influence is the presence of plants and flowers in the schoolroom. These are being increasingly provided both by teachers and Boards, and many schools are really well adorned by their sweet influence. Every school in the land could and should be so brightened and ornamented; for our wild plants, especially ferns, are as effective for this purpose as the cultivated, and being hardy, are more useful than these. Rich folk in both town and country might do much to make our schools beautiful with flowers, by sending plants there, to be kept for a time, and replaced when required; but few of the well-to-do have yet realised this blessed function, this kindly and beautiful service to their less fortunate brethren.

The care of these living creatures, in watering, dusting, ventilating, and tending them, should, as far as possible, be entrusted to the pupils themselves, who really, when interested by proper teaching in these tender and beautiful creations, take great pleasure in doing these educative offices, and to whom it should be made an honour, by wise teachers, to have these entrusted to them.. I am happy to say that many schools are thus well provided with plants, which are carefully tended, and look healthy and blooming — diffusing both beauty and fragrance around them. All depends on the teachers; and though much less is done in this way than might be—and it is painfully small as yet—it is pleasant to note a gradual love and appreciation of these exquisite things.

5. THE STUDY OF EXTERNAL NATURE.— The care of plants *inside* the school at once suggests the wisdom and pleasure of seeking for them *outside*, by the cultivation of a love and study of Nature as an integral part of the regular work of the school. On no point connected with educational reform is Ruskin more eloquent and emphatic than on this. I have already referred to it in some

measure, and I would again, with all the earnestness in my power, plead for Nature being made an essential element in all our education, in every school in the land. Nothing has been more neglected; in nothing have our educational authorities, on whom the conduct of National Education falls, been more blind and backward than in their failure to recognise the importance of outside Nature as a means of health, instruction, training, and higher culture for our children. In most other directions, we have made advances; in many, great if not remarkable progress. In this we may be said to have made none whatever. Here, beyond all question, we have shown reprehensible callousness and blindness to the best interests of the children, in this wonderful and delectable field of human development.

A NEW CRUSADE IN FAVOUR OF TRAINING THROUGH NATURE NEEDED.

This affords only an additional and urgent reason why educational reformers should take the matter up, and institute an active and strenuous crusade, to rouse the attention of the country, and especially of the managers of our educational machinery, to the neglect of Nature in our teaching; and the urgent need of taking our children out of doors, away to the country, for educational ends. It ought not to be left to philanthropic agencies to give our city children a "fresh-air fortnight;" it should be done by our School Boards, as part of their curriculum — to be carried out once a week at least, under the guidance of their teachers—as it will be some happier day. In the department of æsthetic culture, its effects would be remarkable and delightful. In respect to exercise and health, the cultivation of observation and intelligence, and the study of realities as higher than books, to which we are too much in bondage, and in countless other admirable directions, its value and importance are paramount.

It is impossible for any one to speak too strongly in favour of this new and glorious avenue for a higher and broader culture than we yet understand. We *need* the reminder. We ought as a people to take practical action in the matter; and it is with this direct aim, that I here press the subject on all those to whom it should be a labour of love to do it, to help in this way to initiate a broader and sweeter culture for our children, and happier and healthier school life.

6. OTHER ELEMENTS IN ÆSTHETIC TRAINING.—The other means and elements of Æsthetic Education, I can only barely mention. As urged by me in 1874, the Education of Taste is a very broad subject, inasmuch as it should be an element in the culture of every faculty. The *active* education of Taste includes the teaching of form and colour, drawing, and painting, and the principles that guide them; the æsthetic training of the senses and other physical powers; the culture of conduct, person, dress, bearing, manner, and speech; of the intellect, the imagination, the feelings, and the moral faculties; and much more— all which ought to be systematically given in our schools.*

* Report of Committee of Council on Education in Scotland for 1874.

IV.—THE MORAL EFFECTS OF ÆSTHETIC CULTURE.

The effect of this Æsthetic training, among other things, on *Morals* is much greater than may by many be supposed—certainly much greater than we have yet understood, as proved by its neglect. We must rise to the conception advocated six centuries ago in Greece, and embodied in all Plato's teaching. With him, true Art was the best means for the cultivation of Moral character; the soul rising to the Good through the Beautiful, the words καλὸς καὶ ἀγαθος—the Beautiful and the Good —being constantly associated in the teaching of the old philosophers, a union which we are to-day too apt to despise or to deny, certainly too much to neglect. Our own Ruskin once more puts this union with his accustomed force and felicity:

"How can we sufficiently estimate the effect on the mind of a noble youth, at a time when the world opens to him, of having faithful and touching representations put before him of the acts and presences of great men —how many a resolution, which would alter and exalt the whole course of his after-life, might be formed; when, in some dreamy twilight, he met, through his own tears, the fixed eyes of those shadows of the great dead, unescapable and calm, piercing to his soul; or fancied that their lips moved in dread reproof or soundless exhortation? And if but for one out of many, this were true—if yet, in a few, you could be sure that such influence had indeed changed their thoughts and destinies, and turned the eager and reckless youth, who would have cast away his energies on the racehorse or the gambling-table, to that noble *life-race*, that holy *life-*hazard, which should win all glory to himself and all good to his country—would not that, to some purpose, be 'political economy of art'?"*

WHAT SHOULD BE DONE?

Do not, however, let us attempt or expect too much in any efforts we may undertake in this national training of Taste. All real and solid development is necessarily slow, and in

* *A Joy for Ever*, § 108.

no department slower than here. But there is one thing at which we may steadily and successfully aim—to produce a definite conviction in the more enlightened members of the community, that Æsthetic Education should be as much an integral daily element of Public Education as any of the lower subjects now recognised. It is assuredly and sadly true, as John Stuart Mill said, that "it deserves to be regarded in a more serious light than is the custom of these countries." Beyond all doubt or cavil, Æsthetic training in all our schools, elementary and advanced, as much for the rich as for the poor, is, as it has been truly characterised, "the void in modern education." And when that void is filled up, the school will raise national taste and Æsthetic culture more generally, speedily, and effectually than any other agency that exists in the land.

Note.—We *are* moving! In May last an influential deputation from the Committee of the Manchester Art Museum waited upon Mr. Acland, the virtual Minister of Education, contending, among other things, that visits to museums, historical buildings, and botanical gardens, under efficient teachers, formed a valuable branch of education, and asking that time thus spent should be reckoned as if spent in school;

several important School Boards expressing themselves in favour of the request. Mr. Acland, in reply, spoke of the need of making school bright and attractive, and of teaching children to appreciate beautiful things. He would like to see school walls filled with reproductions of friezes and pictures, which would be an education in form and colour; he heartily held the idea of William Morris, that, no more than education, than liberty itself, should art be for the few; and he pledged himself to carry out the wishes of the deputation in the New Code. (See *Journal of Education* for June 1894, p. 324.)

PART THIRD

MORAL EDUCATION IN SCHOOLS

MORALITY A CONSTANT ELEMENT IN ALL
RUSKIN'S TEACHING.

No social reformer of our time has surpassed Ruskin in the wisdom, constancy, and earnestness of his pleading for the Moral element in all culture, in all national, domestic, and social life. Indeed, he has insisted on its presence and activity in spheres and subjects which are popularly, and by many philosophically, supposed to have, if any, only a distant connection with Morals—as in Art, Painting, and Architecture. It is the most distinctive feature of his Social and Æsthetic philosophy, that he advocates Morality as a *constant and essential* principle in *all* artistic and national life; and here also he has done eminent and important service to a much neglected part of National Education, its Moral and Religious side.

I.—THE PRESENT CONDUCT OF MORAL EDUCATION UNSATISFACTORY.

This Moral and Religious portion of Education is popularly supposed to be more carefully provided for than any other in our scholastic system, receiving, it is thought, special attention from the teachers, and being under the fostering care of the clergy. One chief function of the churches ought certainly to be to see to its efficient and punctual teaching. Yet it is the simple truth to say, that no part of our educational work is less *systematically* and less effectively carried out than this same Moral and Religious training, which is supposed to be its best feature. This is a sad and serious fact, which it behoves all educationists and all earnest men to look more seriously into. If its neglect is a fact, it is time, it is more than time, that it should be remedied. This condition of things needs more abundant emphasis than it has received, to draw public attention to its neglect.

All important as Moral Education is acknowledged by all to be, it is in the want of *systematic* teaching that it has been, and still is, defective: even arithmetic, spelling, and writing having surpassed it in both systematic treatment and efficient results.

We have, in this vital and attractive field, *no systematic teaching* of the general principles of conduct; no rousing of the moral nature to strenuous activity by inspiring lessons on the virtues, and on the lives of the best men and women who have exhibited them; nothing done adequately or systematically in this direction at all commensurate with its importance, or comparable with what has been attempted and achieved in the three R's, in mathematics, classics, and other subjects of mere intellectual training.

RUSKIN'S CONDEMNATION OF IT.

The scorn with which Ruskin characterises our Moral and Religious instruction as hitherto given in church and school, is reiterated and often scathing, being uttered at times with volcanic outbursts of sarcasm that need not now detain us. All earnest men who feel the importance of Religion and Morals cannot but be thankful that he has exposed its unsystematic treatment and want of thoroughness. Here is his estimate of our present educational system in relation to its neglect of the Moral element; and of the wonderful possibilities of a thorough system of combined Moral and Intellectual training, in which, as he graphically puts it, it should be our aim "to give to every line of action its unquestioned principle."

"The laws of virtue and honour are," he urges, "to be taught compulsorily to all men; whereas our present forms of education refuse to teach them any; and allow the teaching, by the persons interested in their promulgation, of the laws of cruelty and lying, until we find these British islands gradually filling with a breed of men who cheat without shame, and kill without remorse.

"It is beyond the scope of the most sanguine thought to conceive how much misery and crime would be effaced from the world by persistence, even for a few years, in a system of education directed to raise the fittest into positions of influence, to give to every scale of intellect its natural sphere, and to every line of action its unquestioned principle." *

* *Fors Clavigera*, vol. viii., p. 259.

THE NEED OF BETTER MORAL TRAINING.

Hear Ruskin's courageous exposure of the neglect of Moral Education as compared with the care bestowed on society tinsel. It is a specimen of his indictment, in other respects, of our Moral Education. "You bring up your girls as if they were meant for sideboard ornaments, and then complain of their frivolity. Appeal to the grand instincts of virtue in them; teach them that courage and truth are the pillars of their being. Do you think that they would not answer that appeal, brave and true as they are even now, when you know that there is hardly a girls' school in this Christian kingdom where the children's courage or sincerity would be thought of half so much importance as their way of coming in at a door; and when the whole system of society, as respects the mode of establishing them in life, is one rotten plague of cowardice and imposture—cowardice, in not daring to let them live or love except as their neighbours choose; and imposture, in bringing, for the purposes of our own pride, the full glow of the world's worst vanity upon a girl's eyes, at the very period when the whole happiness of her future existence depends upon her remaining undazzled?"*

II.—THE TEACHING SHOULD BE SYSTEMATIC.

Even with "Religious Knowledge" well taught in our schools, and better taught than it is, Moral teaching and training should be systematically given. That is the position that ought to be pressed home on the attention of all earnest men and women interested, as so many increasingly are, in the moral, social, and religious improvement of the people.

This subject treats of our duties to ourselves and others, their nature, and the principles that regulate their performance. A very large part of error in conduct arises from simple ignorance of the right actions to be done in certain circumstances, and of their results to ourselves and others. We require to know the laws of our constitution and our relations to others, to be able to perform the actions that are in accordance with these. Such truths are in no degree antagonistic to religion, nor are they to be substituted for it. Rightly viewed and

* *Sesame and Lilies*, § 80.

rightly taught, they are its best assistance, materials for its becoming wiser, purer, and nobler. They tell us how to perform the duties incumbent on us, which should be performed religiously and piously.

III.—MORAL TRAINING PARAMOUNT AND FIRST.

With Ruskin, the moral aim of Education is vital, central, and all-embracing—"it is the leading of human souls to what is best, and making what is best out of them,"—an admirable, unsurpassed statement at once of its purpose and its material.

What should be the aim of Education in his eyes? Listen to him:—

"The cry for the education of the lower classes, which is heard every day more widely and more loudly, is a wise and a sacred cry, provided it be extended into one for the education of *all* classes, with definite respect to the work each man has to do, and the substance of which he is made. But it is a foolish and vain cry, if it be understood, as in the plurality of cases it is meant to be, for the expression of mere craving after knowledge, irrespective of the simple purposes of the life that now is, and the blessings of that which is to come."*

THE REAL END OF EDUCATION IS MORAL.

The real object and end of all Education was never better put than by this clear-sighted educational reformer, in a passage which cannot be sufficiently conned and considered by the country; all the more to be noted, now that Education has roused public attention, and commanded so much practical interest, action, and money for its extension and improvement. "Education does not mean," he wisely explains, "teaching people to know what they do not know"—it is not mere instruction, the pouring in of knowledge, however interesting or practically important; it is something much more valuable, more essential to happiness and progress—"it means teaching them to behave as they do not behave. It is not teaching the youth of England the shapes of letters and the tricks of numbers"; —it is not teaching them the three R's, so long, and too long, reckoned the all-in-all

* *Stones of Venice*, vol. iii., App. vii.

of Popular Education — "and then leaving them to turn their arithmetic to roguery and their literature to lust,"—as far as steps have been taken by us to provide against their abuse. "It is," he continues, "training them into the perfect exercise and kingly continence of their bodies and souls—by kindness, by watching, by warning, by precept and by praise—but, above all, by example."*

RUSKIN'S SUMMARY OF ITS AIMS.

He cannot enough emphasise the importance of its Moral elements. "The final results of the education I want you to give your children will be, in a few words, this: They will know what it is to see the sky. They will know what it is to breathe it. And they will know, best of all, what it is to behave under it, as in the presence of a Father who is in heaven."† These words should be carved in letters of gold on the frieze and the pediment of every school in the land, and on the walls of the meeting-room of every School Board in the kingdom.

* *Crown of Wild Olive*, § 144.
† *Fors Clavigera*, vol. i., 1871.

INTELLECTUAL AND MORAL EDUCATION CONTRASTED BY RUSKIN.

"The first," he says, "as indeed the last, nobility of Education is in rule over our thoughts." Again: "Knowledge is not Education, and can neither make us happy nor rich." * Again, in characterising our present Education as devoted too much to intellectual and sordid, worldly aims, he says: "You miss the first letter of your lives, and begin with A for apple-pie, instead of L for love; and the rest of the writing is, some little, some big, some turned the wrong way; and the sum of it all to your perplexity." †

Sir Walter Scott once wrote: "We shall never learn to respect our real calling and destiny till we have taught ourselves to consider everything as moonshine compared with the education of the heart." This is finely echoed by Ruskin:

"In a little while," he truly predicts, "the

---

* *Fors Clavigera*, vol. iii., p. 25.
† *Ibid.*, vol. iii., p. 285.

general interest in Education will assuredly discover that healthy habits, and not mechanical chanting of the church catechism, are the staple of it; and then, not in my model colony only, but as best it can be managed—in un-modelled place or way—girls will be taught to cook, boys to plough, and both to behave; and that with the heart, which is the first piece of all the body to be instructed." *

Again: " All Education must be moral, first; intellectual, secondarily. Intellectual before— much more without—Moral Education is, in completeness, impossible, and, in accomplishment, a calamity." †

Once more, he explains, as already quoted: " I take Wordsworth's single line:

We live by admiration, hope, and love,

for my literal guide in all Education. My final object with every child will be, to teach it what to admire, what to hope for, and what to love." ‡

* *Fors Clavigera*, vol. v., 48.
† *Ibid.*, vol. vi., p. 225.
‡ *Ibid.*, vol. v., 50, p. 30.

HERBART'S TESTIMONY.

In thus emphasising the importance of the systematic teaching of the principles of conduct, Ruskin is in accord with the best educationists of all time; and a glorious anthology of their utterances on the subject could be presented. Let the great German educationist, Herbart, speak for the rest, and concentrate their universal opinions in one passage:

"The one and the whole work of Education may be summed up in the concept—Morality. Morality is usually acknowledged as the *highest* aim of humanity, and consequently of Education." The highest aim of Education with him is in one word, "character-building."

"Since Morality has its place singly and only in the individual's will, founded on right insight, it follows of itself, first and foremost, that the work of Moral Education is not by any means to develop a certain external mode of action, but rather insight, together with corresponding volition, in the mind of the pupil.

"That the idea of the right and good, in all their clearness and purity, may become the essential objects of the will, that the innermost intrinsic contents of the character, the very heart of the personality, shall determine itself according to these ideas, putting back all arbitrary impulses—this and nothing less is the aim of moral culture." *

IV.—THE SUBJECT-MATTER OF SYSTEMATIC MORAL TEACHING.

In urging the teaching of Moral Duty in schools, it is not meant that we are to teach Moral Philosophy. The subject is not to be

---

* Herbart's "Science of Education," p. 111. Surely it is most refreshing and reassuring to find the same noble thoughts echoed by a Vice-President of the Privy Council, the practical head of the Education Department, in his place in Parliament. This was done by Mr. Acland, in his recent memorable speech in introducing the Educational Budget—an epoch-making utterance in such circumstances. After declaring that Mr. Lowe's views on Education were "far too mechanical and inflexible," he said : "Our object is to consider not merely what the children *know* when they leave, but what they *are*, and what they are *to do ;* bearing in mind that the great object is *not merely knowledge, but character.*"

treated technically in form or matter. It makes no inquiry into the nature of the Moral Sense, into theories of the sanction of virtue, and like subjects. It is earnestly and eminently practical, and it is to be as practically taught as writing or arithmetic. As in these subjects, the chief end of our instruction is to show *how to do certain things*, and to exercise in their right performance; so it is in Morals, which is truly the Science of Action—the teaching is to end in action, in doing what has been pointed out, and in correcting errors made in doing it.

The range of subject-matter is wide, varied, and important. For example, amongst *general* truths : It should aim at making children realise the existence of permanent good, yielding truest joy, available to them at all times, beyond mere physical pleasures, which are too exclusively appealed to. It should try to make them feel and follow the joys of right moral action, the sweet delights of doing good. It should seek to show the child that the end of existence here is not so-called "success in life," "getting on in the world"; that this is good and to be valued and pursued, but only as an incidental, not as a final end; and that the true purpose of life lies in the right development of his nature, in the formation of a high, truthful, broad, loving, manly character.

It should teach the child the truth regarding much in action that is misapprehended and misrepresented in common thought and speech: as that "self-denial" is not really self-denial, but rather the choice of a greater good, the renouncing of a lower gratification for a higher, truer, and more lasting joy; and that such words originate in an over-prizing of the physical. It should point out to him that very many of the so-called "ills of life" are self-originated, have their origin in the over-valuing of what is not truly valuable, in the following as certain of what is contingent, the reckoning as permanent of what is evanescent or changeable. Such truths can be simply taught and made plain and clear even to children.

THE CHIEF DUTIES TO BE TAUGHT.

Then the various *duties* of life should be taken up separately, as far as they belong to the life of childhood and boyhood. These require explanation and enforcement; and they form a wide and attractive field.

Amongst duties to ourselves: there are, the regulation of the appetite, cleanliness, temperance, exercise, and the other virtues belonging to physical morality; frankness, firmness, self-service, self-equipoise, courage, energy, presence of mind, perseverance, modesty, contempt of false opinion, resource, manliness, and such like—with their opposite ills and pains.

Amongst duties to others: there are, kindness to animals and to all, forbearance, forgiveness, gentleness, generosity, conscientiousness, reverence, courtesy, honour, truth, heroism, and the like—with their opposite ills and pains. The list is inexhaustible.

The very mention of such a course of instruction and influence is inspiring, and carries with it its own recommendation. The subjects are quite within the grasp of children, and rightly treated, have a natural attraction for the young; and they can be made as fascinating as stories of adventure.

RUSKIN'S EXPOSITION OF THESE.

The *general* elements of the Moral Education which Ruskin wishes to see carried on in all our schools, he thus summarises:—

"Man's use and function are, to be the witness of the glory of God, and to advance that glory, by his reasonable obedience and resultant happiness. People speak in this working age, when they speak from their hearts, as though houses and lands, and food and raiment, were alone useful, and as if sight, thought, and admiration were all profitless. . . .*

"Men's business in this world falls mainly into three divisions:—

"(1) To know themselves, and the existing state of things with which they have to do.

* *Modern Painters*, vol. ii., chap. i., §§ 4, 5.

"(2) To be happy in themselves and the existing state of things, so far as neither are marred or mendable.

"(3) To mend themselves and the existing state of things, so far as either are marred or mendable."*

In *Fors Clavigera*, he thus puts the general elements of moral training :—

"Moral Education begins in making the creature to be educated clean and obedient. This must be done thoroughly and at all cost, and with any kind of compulsion rendered necessary by the nature of the animal, be it dog, child, or man. Moral Education consists in making the creature practically serviceable to other creatures, according to the nature and extent of its own capacities; taking care that it be healthily developed in such service. Moral Education is summed when the creature has been made to do its work with delight and thoroughly." †

* *Modern Painters*, vol. iii., chap. iv., § 2.
† *Fors Clavigera*, vol. vi., p. 225.

V.—HOW TO ACCOMPLISH THESE MORAL AIMS.

To accomplish these high ends in Popular Education, Ruskin tells the means. He holds that—

"There should be training schools for youth, established at government cost, and under government discipline, over the whole country; that every child born in the country should, at the parent's wish, be permitted (and in certain cases be, under penalty, required) to pass through them; and that, in these schools, the child should (with other minor pieces of knowledge) be taught, with the best skill of teaching that the country could produce, the following three things :—

"(*a*) The laws of health, and the exercises enjoined by them;

"(*b*) Habits of gentleness and justice; and

"(*c*) The calling by which he is to live."

MORAL EDUCATION IN SCHOOLS   119

VI.—VIRTUES ON WHICH RUSKIN LAYS STRESS.

There are certain virtues the cultivation of which he emphasises as specially necessary in this country, and as painfully and generally neglected.

Summarising the habits he desires our children to be specially trained in, he says they ought to be taught to be "clean, active, honest, and useful." He wishes to be established all over the land, "Schools of History, Natural History, and Art, such as may enable children to know the meaning of the words, Beauty, Courtesy, Compassion, Gladness, and Religion."*

1. CLEANLINESS.—He thus places cleanliness first in the order of merit. In *Fors*, he repeats it: "The speedy abolition of all abolishable filth is the first process of Education."† All who know the habits of our people, and the condition of our children in this particular, will also set this neglected

* *Fors Clavigera*, vol. iv., p. 204.
† *Ibid.*, vol. vi., p. 225.

virtue in the first rank. Carlyle's *Gospel of Soap* still requires increasingly to be preached over the length and breadth of the land.

2. OBEDIENCE.—On this intellectual and moral habit of mind, Ruskin puts immense, and, as some may deem it, excessive value. Next to cleanliness, he always puts obedience. Our children are to be trained to be " clean and obedient," which is to be done " thoroughly and at all cost," and even " with any kind of compulsion." Indeed, he holds that Religion itself "primarily means obedience"; and he enters on an interesting etymological proof that this is so—its chief function, according to its name, being to *bind* mankind *back* from a rebellious use of its natural tendencies.*

3. KINDNESS TO ANIMAL LIFE.—Nothing secures the earnest pleadings of Ruskin's heart and pen more than this neglected virtue

---

* From Lat. *re*, back, and *ligo*, to bind. See *Fors Clavigera*, vol. iv., p. 204. In the Codes of the Education Department, the grants for Discipline are made on condition that the Inspector is satisfied with "the behaviour of the children, their cleanliness and obedience, and their honesty under examination."

—talked about, certainly, but little practised in either town or country. He places it on its true pedestal when he calls it "piety": that is, he holds that love to God and love to His lower creatures are truly the same, and should be taught together as equally binding. The one should be made the best evidence of the other, as much as love to our fellow-men is of love of God. "Education," says he, "rightly apprehended, consists, half of it, in making children familiar with natural objects, and the other half in teaching the practice of piety towards them (piety meaning kindness to living things and orderly use of the lifeless)."*

4. HONESTY.—In Ruskin's eyes, this seemingly commonplace virtue is one of the very rarest in character and social life ; although it is the basis of all individual and national happiness and amelioration of our condition. Its want is, he thinks, the source of nine-tenths of the social and economic miseries under which we now groan ; and its teaching and practice would go far to remove them. On these, he

* *Fors Clavigera*, vol. viii., p. 253.

lays the strongest emphasis, and devotes large space to expound the high position he gives to the neglected virtue of Honesty, which he always includes in his statement of the grand aims of Moral Training.

He does this with special force in his celebrated preface to *Unto this Last*,—the papers which embody more of his peculiar Political Economy than any other, and which roused such fierce antagonism that their publication in the *Cornhill*, in 1860, was stopped:

"Their second object was to show that the acquisition of wealth was finally possible only under certain moral conditions of society, of which quite the first was a belief in the existence, and even for practical purposes, in the attainability of honesty. Without venturing to pronounce, since on such a matter human judgment is by no means conclusive, what is, or is not the noblest of God's works, we may yet admit so much of Pope's assertion as that an honest man is among His best works presently visible, and, as things stand, a somewhat rare, but not an incredible or miraculous, work, still less an abnormal one.

"I have sometimes heard Pope condemned

for the lowness instead of the height of his standard. Honesty is indeed a respectable virtue, but how much higher may men attain! Shall nothing more be asked of us than that we be honest? For the present, good friends, nothing. It seems that, in our aspirations to be more than that, we have, to some extent, lost sight of the propriety of being so much as that. What else we may have lost faith in, there shall be here no question; but, assuredly, we have lost faith in common honesty, and in the working power of it. And this faith, with the facts on which it may rest, is quite our first business to recover and keep." *

VII.—VIRTUES SPECIALLY EMPHASISED BY RUSKIN.

In carrying out the Moral Education of our children, there are some elements in it which Ruskin elaborates more fully, and on which it behoves us, if we are wise, to bestow more attention.

* But see the whole passage and argument in the Preface to *Unto this Last*.

Several motives, for example, much employed in Education by teachers and others as impulses to work, which are detrimental to high moral life, Ruskin would have us strenuously guard against.

1. INTELLECTUAL AND SOCIAL HUMILITY.—He wisely counsels us to "enforce on every scholar's heart, from the first to the last stage of his instruction, the irrevocable ordinance that his mental rank among men is fixed from the hour he was born; that, by no temporary or violent effort, can he train, though he may seriously injure, the faculties he has; that, by no manner of effort, can he increase them; and that his best happiness is to consist in the admiration of powers by him for ever unattainable, and of arts and deeds by him for ever inimitable."

He strongly condemns "the personal conceit and ambition in minds of selfish activity, which lead to the disdain of manual labour, and the desire of all sorts of unattainable things, and fill the streets with discontented and useless persons seeking some means of living in town society by their wits. Every reader's experience," he says, "must avow the extent and increasing plague of this fermenting imbecility, striving to make for itself what it calls a 'position in life.'"

He tells us that one of the most difficult questions connected with Education is "the mode in which the chance of advancement in life is to be extended to all, and yet made compatible with contentment in the pursuit of lower avocations by those whose abilities do not qualify them for the higher."*

"What is chiefly needed in England at the present day," he further explains, "is to show the quantity of pleasure that may be obtained by a consistent, well-administered competence, modest, confessed and laborious. We need examples of people who, leaving Heaven to decide whether they are to rise in the world, decide for themselves whether they will be happy in it, and have resolved to seek, not greater wealth, but simpler pleasure, not higher fortune, but deeper felicity; making the first of possessions self-possession, and honouring themselves in the harmless pride and calm pursuits of peace." †

* *A Joy for Ever*, § 135.   † *Unto this Last*, § 83.

He would specially teach "to all children, of whatever gift, grade, or age, the virtue of Humility, as including all the habits of Obedience and instincts of Reverence," which are dwelt on throughout *Fors*, and in all his other books. "The aphorism cannot be too often repeated," he urges, "that Moral Education begins in making the creature we have to educate clean and obedient. In after time, this 'virtue of humility' is to be taught to a child by gentleness to its failures, showing it that by reason of its narrow powers it cannot but fail."

ILLUSTRATION FROM HIS OWN SCHOOL DAYS.

"I have seen my old clerical master, the Rev. Thomas Dale," he tells us, in illustration, "beating his son Tom hard over the head with the edge of a grammar, because Tom could not construe a Latin verse; when the reverend gentleman ought only with extreme tenderness and pitifulness to have explained to Tom that—he wasn't Thomas the Rhymer."

"But it is to be remembered," he goes on to

point out, "that Humility can only be truly, and therefore only effectively taught when the master is swift to recognise the special faculties of children, no less than their weaknesses; that it is his quite highest and most noble function to discern these, and prevent their discouragement or effacement in the vulgar press for a common prize." *

2. REVERENT ADMIRATION.—We have seen how, in taking Wordsworth as his guide in the Education he wishes for all our boys and girls, — "we live by admiration, hope, and love;"—Admiration comes first. He makes it also his "final object," to teach "what to admire." He further explains this, and returns to it a hundred times in his writings.

"A man's happiness consists," he truly says, "infinitely more in admiration of the faculties of others than in confidence of his own. Reverent admiration is the perfect human gift in him; all lower animals are happy and noble in the degree they can share it. A dog reverences you, a fly does not; the capacity of partly understanding a

* *Fors Clavigera*, vol. viii., p. 238.

creature above him is the dog's nobility. Increase such admiration in human beings, and you increase daily their happiness, peace, and dignity; take it away, and you make them wretched as well as vile. But for fifty years back, modern education has devoted itself simply to the teaching of impudence; and then we complain that we can no more manage our mobs." *

As he elsewhere in *Fors* says, Moral education cannot be efficiently carried out, "until some degree of Intellectual education has been given also."

What does this *Intellectual* education mainly consist in, according to this educationist? Chiefly in certain *moral* elements!

"Intellectual Education," he continues, "consists in giving the creatures the faculties of admiration, hope, and love." †

Do let the country, and especially our educationists, take careful note that both the basis and means of *Intellectual* education lie in the training of these *Moral* faculties; and that the foremost and most essential is Admiration — perception of and joy in the

* *Fors*, vol. i. 9, p. 9.   † *Ibid.*, vol. vi. 225.

greatness of others, in all in which they are above us in faculty and achievement.

How is this training to be accomplished? According to the same teacher, in three special fields, on which volumes could and should be written, in correction of our present narrow and barren procedure, but which can here be only enumerated.

"These are to be taught by the study of beautiful Nature; the sight and history of noble persons; and the setting forth of noble objects of action."*

The importance of Admiration in human education and social progress is based on the fact of the irreversible inequalities that exist in the faculties of all creatures, and not less of mankind.

"My continual aim," says Ruskin, emphasising Carlyle, "has been to show the eternal superiority of some men to others, sometimes even of one man to all others; and to show also the advisability of appointing such persons or person to guide, to lead, or, on occasion, even compel and subdue, their inferiors, according to their better knowledge and wiser will."

* *Fors*, vol. vi., p. 225.

3. EMULATION CONDEMNED.—There is one test of capacity in children which, in common with all true educationists, Ruskin emphatically and indignantly repudiates and condemns—that is Emulation. He returns to the subject repeatedly, and speaks with highest wisdom.

"In all trial of our children, I believe all Emulation to be a false motive, and all giving of prizes a false means. All that you can depend upon in a boy, as significative of true power, likely to issue in good fruit, is his will to work for the work's sake, not his desire to surpass his schoolfellows; and the aim of the teaching you give him ought to be to prove to him, and strengthen in him, his own separate gift, not to puff him into swollen rivalry with those who are everlastingly greater than he: still less ought you to hang favours and ribands about the neck of the creature who is the greatest, to make the rest envy him. Try to make them love him and follow him, not struggle with him.

"There must, of course, be examination, to ascertain and attest both progress and relative capacity; but our aim should be to make the students rather look upon it as a means of ascertaining their own true positions and powers in the world, than as an arena in which to carry away a present victory."*

NO COMPETITION TO BE ALLOWED.

Here is another of his telling utterances:—

"Of schools in all places, and for all ages, the healthy working will depend on the total exclusion of the stimulus of Competition in any form or disguise. Every child should be measured by its own standard, trained to its own duty, and rewarded by its just praise. It is the effort that deserves praise, not the success; nor is it a question for any student whether he is cleverer than others or duller, but whether he has done the best he could with the gifts he has."†

Righteously indignant, he exclaims: "The madness of the modern cram and examination system arises principally out of the struggle to get lucrative places, but partly also out of the

---
* *A Joy for Ever*, §§ 135–6.
† *Fors Clavigera*, vol. viii., p. 255.

radical blockheadism of supposing that all men are naturally equal and can only make their way by elbowing: the facts being that every child is born with an accurately defined and absolutely limited capacity; that he is naturally (if able at all) able for some things and unable for others; that no effort and no teaching can add one particle to the granted ounces of his available brains; that by competition, he may paralyse or pervert his faculties, but cannot stretch them a line; and that the entire grace, happiness, and virtue of his life depend on his contentment in doing what he can dutifully, and in staying where he is peaceably. So far as regards the less or more capacity of others, his superiorities are to be used for *their* help, not for his own pre-eminence; and his inferiorities to be no ground of mortification, but of pleasure in the admiration of nobler powers."*

"Over the door of every school, and the gate of every college, I would fain see engraved in their marble, the Absolute Forbidding,

μηδὲν κατὰ ἐρίθειαν ἢ κενοδοξίαν,

* *Fors*, vol. viii., p. 255.

—'Let *nothing* be done through strife or vain glory:' and I would have fixed, for each age of children and students, a certain standard of pass in examination, so adapted to average capacity and power of exertion that none need fear who had attended to their lessons and obeyed their masters; while its variety of trial should yet admit of the natural distinctions attaching to progress in especial subjects and skill in peculiar arts. Beyond such indication or acknowledgment of merit, there should be neither prizes nor honours; these are meant by Heaven to be the proper rewards of a man's consistent, and kindly life, not of a youth's temporary and selfish exertion."*

THE TRUE PURPOSE OF EXAMINATIONS.

These are sound and suggestive counsels, which wise lovers of their kind, whether educationists or not, have ever pleaded for, but to which we have as yet turned deaf ears and hard and selfish hearts, to the serious detriment of our children and of national morality. Our present almost universal practice ministers

Fors, vol. viii., p. 255.

painfully to vanity and selfishness. Moreover, it results in maintaining a lower level of attainment and work, because it is judged not by absolute, but only relative, merit. As has been wittily and wisely said, our aim ought to be, to generate in our children "a desire for *excellence*, not for *excelling*." Horace Mann, the great American educationist, and one of the most enlightened the world has seen, puts this subject in a phrase—"We are all anti-emulation men—that is, all against any system of rewards and prizes designed to withdraw the mind from the comparison of itself with a standard of excellence, and to substitute a rival for that standard."*

HOW SHOULD EMULATION BE USED?

The right use of Emulation, or the natural Love of Approbation, which is possessed by all human beings, is one of the most difficult practical problems in the training of a child. But there is no doubt whatever that, in our past and present practice, we have abused its

* *Education: its Principles and Practice as developed by George Combe*, edited by William Jolly (Macmillan), p. 389.

potency, and fostered it to painful strength, rather than wisely utilised its legitimate and useful power; and have thus raised a crop of dangerous moral weeds which it will take generations to eradicate.

VIII.—EDUCATION SHOULD TEACH THE TRUE MEANING OF WEALTH.

In endeavouring to realise a higher type of personal and social existence, it is all important, according to Ruskin, to understand clearly in what Wealth really consists. On this subject, he has done eminent service for the Educationist, the social reformer, and the economist, by elaborately, earnestly, philosophically, and eloquently giving its true definition. Wealth does not mean mere possession; much less is it mere riches. Wealth consists in "the possession of the valuable by the valiant." "There is no wealth but life; life including all its powers of love, joy, and admiration. That country is the richest which nourishes the greatest number of noble and happy human beings; that man is the richest who, having perfected the functions of his own life to the utmost, has also the widest helpful influence, both personal and by means of his possessions, over the lives of others."

We are, and have been, altogether wrong in our estimate of Wealth, and the result has been national and individual misery. We have confounded Wealth with money-massing, instead of realising that it truly and literally signifies well-being; and "the attraction of riches is," in consequence of this false estimate and false teaching, "too strong, as their authority is too weighty for the reason of mankind." This evil estimate influences and corrupts not only the individual life but all our social system; it vitiates all our Political and Social Economy, as at present taught in our dominant treatises and schools. One of Ruskin's chief aims, in his Economical works, is to overturn this radical misconception in regard to Wealth, and replace it by something truer and higher. If our teaching in this respect were what it ought to be—

"Perhaps it may even appear," as this strange political economist says, "after some consideration that the persons themselves are the Wealth—that these pieces of gold with which we are in the habit of guiding them are, in fact, nothing more than a kind of Byzantine harness or trappings, very glittering and beautiful in barbaric sight, wherewith we bridle the creatures; but that if these same living creatures could be guided without the fretting and jingling of the Byzants in their mouths and ears, they might themselves be more valuable than their bridles. In fact, it may be discovered that the true veins of Wealth are purple, and not in rock but in flesh—perhaps even that the final outcome and consummation of all Wealth is in producing as many as possible, full-breathed, bright-eyed, and happy-hearted human creatures.

"Our modern Wealth I think has rather a tendency the other way; most political economists appearing to consider multitudes of human creatures not conducive to Wealth, or at best conducive to it only by remaining in a dim-eyed and narrow-chested state of being.

"Nevertheless it is open, I repeat, to serious question, which I leave to the reader's pondering, whether among national manufactures, that of souls of a good quality may not at last turn out a quite leadingly lucrative one?

"Nay, in some far away and yet undreamt of hour, I can even imagine that England may cast all thoughts of possessive wealth back to the barbaric nations among whom they first arose, and that, while the sands of the Indus and adamant of Golconda may yet stiffen the housings of the charger, and flash from the turban of the slave, she, as a Christian mother, may at last attain to the virtues and the treasures of a heathen one, and be able to lead forth her sons, saying,—"These are my jewels." *

EDUCATION SHOULD FURNISH A CHILD WITH A PLAN OF LIFE.

A root idea always present to Ruskin, in speaking of Education, as to all true educators, is, what life truly is, and how Education can be so conducted as to enable us to take the most out of it, by leading to Spencer's "complete living." As Ruskin again and again says: "Whatever advantages we possess in the present day, in the diffusion of Education and of literature, can only be rightly used by

* *Unto this Last*, §§ 40–41.

any of us, when we have apprehended clearly what Education is to lead to, and literature to teach.*

Pestalozzi put the whole in a nut-shell, with equal philosophy and point, when he said: "The ultimate end of Education is, not perfection in the accomplishments of the school, (as they are most generally made), but *fitness for life*."

Froebel did the same less briefly, but not less wisely: "What is the purpose of Education?" he asks. His answer is: "Man lives in a world of objects which influence him, and which he desires to influence; therefore, he ought to know these objects in their nature, in their conditions, and in their relations with each other and with mankind." †

Huxley has an admirable passage in his "Lay Sermons," in which life is compared to a game of chess, on the winning or losing of which our happiness wholly depends; and Education, to the learning of the rules of that game.

George Combe long ago pleaded for and expounded the need of giving children

* *Sesame and Lilies*, § 51.   † Froebel's *Autob.*, p. 69.

"correct views of the real principles, machinery and objects of life, and of training them to act systematically in relation to them in their habitual conduct," as an essential part of Education, whatever else was given or omitted, and he compared life to a voyage of adventure, on which most of us at present embark "without knowledge of its navigation, without charts, and without any particular port of destination in view;" and he held that "by correct and enlarged knowledge of human nature and of the external world, the young might be furnished with a chart and plan of life suited to their wants, desires, and capacities as rational beings." *

Ruskin has a similar passage, in which he characterises Education as the means of gaining or losing an estate : †

"Suppose," says he, "I were able to call at this moment to any one in the audience by name, and to tell him positively that I knew a large estate had been lately left to him on some curious conditions; but that, though I

---

* *Education*, &c., by George Combe, in which the subject is very fully treated. See Index.
† *Sesame and Lilies*, § 108.

knew it was large, I did not know how large, nor even where it was—whether in the East Indies or the West, or in England, or at the Antipodes. I only knew it was a vast estate, and that there was a chance of his losing it altogether if he did not soon find out on what terms it had been left to him. Suppose I were able to say this positively to any single man in this audience, and he knew that I did not speak without warrant, do you think that he would rest content with that vague knowledge, if it were anywise possible to obtain more? Would he not give every energy to find some trace of the facts, and never rest till he had ascertained where this place was, and what it was like? And suppose he were a young man, and all he could discover by his best endeavour was, that the estate was never to be his at all, unless he persevered, during certain years of probation, in an orderly and industrious life; but that, according to the rightness of his conduct, the portion of the estate assigned to him would be greater or less, so that it literally depended on his behaviour from day to day whether he got ten thousand a year, or thirty thousand a year, or nothing whatever—would you not think it strange if the youth never troubled himself to satisfy the conditions in any way, nor even to know what was required of him, but lived exactly as he chose, and never enquired whether his chances of the estate were increasing or passing away? Well, you know that this is actually and literally so with the greater number of the educated persons now living in Christian countries. Nearly every man and woman in such a company as this, outwardly professes to believe—and a large number unquestionably think they believe—much more than this; not only that a quite unlimited estate is in prospect for them if they please the Holder of it, but that the infinite contrary of such a possession — an estate of perpetual misery—is in store for them if they displease this great Land-Holder, this great Heaven-Holder. And yet there is not one in a thousand of these human souls that cares to think, for ten minutes of the day, where this estate is, or how beautiful it is, or what kind of life they are to lead in it, or what kind of life they must lead to obtain it."

Thirteen years ago I pressed this idea of our so conducting the education of a child as to enable him to know *himself* and his *environment*—and the *duties* thence arising, as a necessary preparation for life—in these terms:*—" Here is man, a delicately organised being, possessing a certain physical and mental constitution, ushered into a wonderful system of beings, objects, and forces, of countless variety and intricacy, which are governed by certain irrevocable laws dispensing to him happiness or misery with absolute certainty and without compunction, according to the obedience he renders to them, from which ignorance is no safeguard, and with which suffering is no plea. These laws are universal, irreversible, and undiscriminating; and the systems of things regulated by them are ever around him, press upon him, and pervade him in social and mental, as certainly as in physical, matters, and deal out pleasure or pain to him, whether he knows them intelligently or not; and his whole life, from the innermost recesses of his personal and domestic relations to the most distant influences of the stars, is swayed

* *Education Review* (Boston, U.S.A., July 1881).

by them with omnipotent power from the cradle to the grave. In such circumstances, in view of the plain facts of the case, what would seem to be the wise and sensible course for parents and teachers to pursue in regard to the child? Surely to give him some knowledge of himself and his all-regulating surroundings, in order to prepare him as fully as possible for entering into this great system of things, so pregnant with his bliss or bane; that he may know, as far as he can, the conditions of his existence, the rules of the mighty game he has to play. Surely he ought to be prepared for the voyage of life,—have a chart of the course to be steered, the rocks and shoals to be avoided, the winds and storms to be encountered; that he may escape danger or shipwreck for himself and those he holds dearest, and damage and wrong to others.

"Such a preparation for life seems at once dictated by common sense, sound philosophy, enlightened selfishness, and the highest sanctions."

Hence Ruskin recommends that we should know ourselves "the cunning of our right hand, the capabilities of our brain, the excellencies and ailments of our moral nature, and the existing state of things we have to do with." No matter how difficult, this knowledge should be gained: "ignorance is death." On this knowledge of our surroundings, rests the possibility of improvement and the possession of permanent happiness and peace.

IX.—THE TEACHING OF SOCIAL AND POLITICAL ECONOMY.

Our happiness is determined by the state of the society in which we have to live, the Social and Political elements that form the Commonwealth in which we are placed. To make the most of these, to escape the evils and to win the possible pleasures of the case, we ought to be taught the nature of the social system we enter into; we ought to know "the existing state of things we have to do with," as Ruskin puts it. He holds that the great evil of life is threefold, in—

"First—Man's ignorance of himself and the existing state of things he has to do with.

"Second—Man's misery in himself and the existing things he has to do with.

"Third — Man's inclination to let himself and the existing state of things he has to do with alone; at least in the way of correction.

"To rectify these, the future man must know himself and his surroundings; with all this knowledge, he will have no guarantee for success or happiness in his work. Therefore, an essential portion of his preparatory education is careful instruction in Social and Political Economy."

ITS PAST NEGLECT.

He says that "the want of this instruction which hitherto has disgraced our Schools and Universities, has indeed been the cause of ruin or total inutility of life to multitudes of our men of estate. This deficiency in our public Education," he assures us, "cannot exist much longer. Only we must see that our rich men take their standing more firmly than they have done hitherto, as to the right use of wealth; for the position of a rich man is generally contemplated by Political Economists as being precisely the reverse of what it ought to be."*

* *A Joy for Ever*, § 143.

RUSKIN'S POLITICAL ECONOMY.

This " Moral and Political teaching " should, of course, be founded on "the most perfect possible analysis of the results of human conduct." Ruskin's analysis differs radically from that of our recognised and dominant teachers, and forms the burden of "The New Political Economy" which it has been the main business of his life to preach, in season and out of season, and for which he has received such vituperation on the one side, and admiration on the other. He has fullest confidence in the wisdom of his own teaching, and holds that it contains "the first true system of Political Economy which has been published in England," as originally given in his *Munera Pulveris*.

WILLIAM ELLIS'S WORK IN THIS EDUCATIONAL FIELD.

The most enlightened and systematic attempt ever tried in this country towards basing education on the teaching of Moral and Social Science, was made by the late William

Ellis, the founder of the Birkbeck Schools in London, whose "Life"* has lately been published, and who spent more than half-a-million in a life-long endeavour to reduce it to practice in school teaching; of which I have elsewhere given some account.† His utterances are finely akin to those of Ruskin.

Education with him meant, "An earnest application of well-selected means to impart to all, such a knowledge of the laws of the universe, especially of their practical bearing upon the daily wants and business of life, as that all may be clearly convinced that their happiness is only to be attained by placing themselves in harmony with those laws; to communicate to all, such manual, muscular, and intellectual dexterity as may qualify them to gain, extend, add to, and improve their knowledge, and appropriate and apply it; and also to implant those habits of observation, application, and forethought,

* See *Life of William Ellis*, by E. K. Blythe—an important work, too little known.
† In *Education: its Principles and Practice as developed by George Combe*, edited by William Jolly (Macmillan), (see Index—Ellis; and p. 236 for list of his works); and in *Good Words*, 1887.

without which the soundest intellectual acquirements are comparatively useless."*

According to Ellis, "A people so educated would be inspired, not with the mere vulgar notion of 'getting on,' not with the vain illusory desire of 'rising in the world,' but with a solemn sense of the sacredness of every duty undertaken, of every contract entered into. And thus the desire of happiness and gratification, the motive force of our conduct, and exertion would be subjugated and regulated by an all-pervading sense of duty, and thereby be rendered more capable of gaining its end."†

Ellis's great and peculiar contribution to educational philosophy was his advocacy of the need of imparting to the young in school, a knowledge of the principles of *combined* Moral and Social Science, which he called "the Conditions of Human Well-being." On these, he wrote and published a long and important series, the last being called *Religion in Common Life*, after Principal Caird's celebrated sermon. This subject is a daily, integral part of the teaching in the schools

* See Ellis's "Life." † *Ibid.*

he established, the Birkbeck Schools, in London, and others founded on their model. One of these is conducted away down in Dorset, in the country town of Blandford, by a friend of Ellis's, and George Combe's, Mr. Horlock Bastard, in whose school, among other things, corporal punishment is unknown.*

THE SUBJECT BEGINS TO BE RECOGNISED.

A sign of the times, in this combined Moral and Economic direction, by which such instruction is coming more and more to be systematically given in many schools, is the recent publication of the *Citizen Reader* and *Laws of Every Day Life*, by Arnold-Foster, and similar works, in which these topics, which are generally thought abstruse, are treated with simplicity and interest.

A still more encouraging fact is that the subject is recognised and paid for, according to a well-put programme, in the new Code recently issued for Evening and

* See Combe's *Education*, &c., chap. vii., for an account of the pioneer educational efforts of these and like-minded workers, including that very remarkable man, William Lovett.

Continuation Schools, under the Education Department.*

Though the doctrines in most of such books are not according to the mind of Ruskin, their very use in schools is a practical acknowledgment of the truth of Ruskin's contention, that Education should furnish the child with "the conditions of his existence, the rules of the mighty game he has to play."

X.—THE SYSTEMATIC TEACHING OF MORAL DUTY SHOULD BE UNIVERSAL.

The foregoing are but fragments of Ruskin's powerful and eloquent utterances regarding the need and primary importance of Moral Training in all school life and teaching. If these were all gathered and classified, they would form a large and valuable addition to our educational literature, all the more valuable that they emphasise, and give admirable suggestions on, comparatively neglected elements in our common school teaching.

Surely, therefore, in view of all that has

* Under the National Home Reading Union, the study of the "Life and Duties of the Citizen" is also fostered.

been said, Moral Duty, the Conduct of Life, the Rules of Right Living—by whatever name the subject may be called—ought to be taught in all our schools, and ought to be taught regularly and systematically.

THE MEANS OF DOING IT.

The teacher should himself traverse the whole field and select the portions suitable to his pupils. A part of every day ought to be spent at the subject; at least, it should be taught several times a week. Each lesson should be short, and it should be given clearly and pleasantly, and chiefly by well-selected examples, told or read, and set in their true light. False or low opinions on any portion should be carefully pointed out. A high, but not Utopian, standard should be maintained. Lecturing is, of course, to be avoided: the subject cannot be made to influence life by didactic and moral sermonising, but by teaching and explaining in a loving, earnest spirit, that speaks through accent, word, manner, and mode of treatment.

THE INFLUENCE OF SUCH TEACHING.

The influence of such a course on the school tone would be very great. It would create a sweeter and higher moral atmosphere. It would certainly lessen punishment; for with such a standard, with such grand and kindly themes, mere corporal pain would be less, if at all, required. The results of such a scheme, rightly taught, would be, the formation in the children of true opinion on moral action, good habits of life, and high tone. It should generate in the hearts of the young a supreme and ardent love of truth and goodness, which would go with them for ever, and be a central impulse throughout life, impelling towards noble character. Can we estimate the extent and strength of the influence a good teacher could wield in this way, in the daily school life, home life, world life, of his pupils, and, through them, on society and on the coming generations? The great possibility of being the centre of such influence is not the inheritance of every man—it is that of the teacher. Can any true and good teacher hesitate to try to become something of this? "If life be a battle, then let the teacher be a bard, inspiring his boys for it with martial music," as Jean Paul Richter says.

IT IS PARTIALLY RECOGNISED BY THE EDUCATION DEPARTMENT.

In the Codes of the Education Department, this subject has been tacitly, if not expressly, recognised and encouraged. In both the Scotch and English Codes, these important and well-put suggestions occur: "To meet the requirement respecting discipline, the managers and teachers will be expected to satisfy the inspector that all reasonable care is taken in the ordinary management of the school, to bring up the children in the habits of punctuality, of good manners and language, of cleanliness and neatness, and also to impress upon the children the importance of cheerful obedience to duty, of consideration and respect for others, and of honour and truthfulness in word and act." *

* Art. 19, A.

IT SHOULD BE EXTENDED AND SYSTE-MATICALLY TAUGHT.

What I here plead for is, that managers and teachers, thus addressed, should take up the subject more earnestly and *systematically* than they have yet done, and make it an *integral* and *daily* portion of the teaching and training of the school; at least, as much and as carefully done as any one of the staple subjects of school training and instruction. They have in many cases risen admirably to the occasion in other subjects recommended; and if they did the same with this, the results would be delightful and gratifying to all concerned, and would initiate a new Reformation.

TEXT-BOOKS FOR THE TEACHING OF THE SUBJECT.

Such a course can be given with ease and pleasure, and with little trouble to the teacher; though, surely, its nature and influence are more than enough to repay much trouble and study, if required. Text-books are needed on this subject, as in all others;

but, I am sorry to say, they are fewer in number in this all-important field than in any other. While thousands of class-books have been produced for the "beggarly elements" of instruction, they are sparse, and many of them more or less imperfect, in regard to this the highest object of all training. We require two classes of books for efficient teaching—one for the teacher's use, and one for his pupils'; a fact true of all subjects, though too little acted on by purveyors of school-books.

For the use of *teachers*, I would mention Ruskin's own works, which are invaluable for this purpose; Professor Blackie's *Self Culture*, fresh, attractive, and inspiring; and Charles Bray's *Education of the Feelings*, full of wise counsel and direction regarding the cultivation of all the elements of character—both of these last being cheap and simple, thoroughly good and helpful. Books of illustrative examples are also needed by the teacher. The common reading-books often supply these; and abundant materials may be found in Smiles' *Self Help* and *Character;* Miss Yonge's *Book of Golden Deeds* and *Book of Worthies;* Chambers'

Moral Class Book; the *Percy Anecdotes;* Hackwood's *Lessons on Moral Subjects* (Nelson), and Prescott's *Moral Education.*

Of books to be put into the *children's* hands, there are, alas, few, and these often objectionable. Out of sight, the best in the field is Mrs. Charles Bray's *Elements of Morality* (Longmans), in which the chief duties are traversed, in principle and detail, in small space, with winning simplicity, elevated tone, and admirable style. It is a book that ought daily to be in the hands of every parent, teacher, and child in the land. I would also recommend *Helps for the Young in their Efforts at Self-Guidance,* edited by the Rev. W. Jowitt (Longmans), which was written by William Ellis, and a small and simple handbook by the Rev. R. Lawson of Maybole, *Good Manners for Boys and Girls, in School, at Home, and Out of Doors.**

XI.—AUXILIARY AIDS TO MORAL TRAINING IN SCHOOL.

There are certain auxiliaries to the Moral Training of our children, which might be more

* Published by Parlane, Paisley (½d. each or 4d. per dozen).

looked on in that light, and utilised for that purpose in schools. Some of these I would briefly refer to :—

1. POETRY FOR RECITATION.—The selection made is often paltry and thin, if it does not embody sentiments that are beyond children's possible experience; introducing them prematurely to emotions that should be barred from youthful thoughts, or appealing to feelings that are objectionable in a moral point of view.

PIECES TO BE AVOIDED.

For example, to take a mild case, the "Combat between Fitz-James and Roderick Dhu,"* once universal in schools, is a poetical and powerful presentation of a duel to the death, with an all too vivid and realistic picture of fierce blood-thirstiness, and, in the end, a tiger-like struggle to kill, in a pool of human gore. I ask all to consider if such representations of the brutal passions, here made all the more intense through the

* In Sir Walter Scott's *Lady of the Lake*.

skill of the poet, is desirable reading for young children. To learn it and prepare it minutely in meaning and association, is it not still more objectionable, to say the least of it? Surely, surely something better can be chosen than this powerful but repellent theme. We have, however, become so accustomed to it that we have ceased to see the matter in its true moral relations. Happily, of late years, this passage, savouring too much of the sensationalism of modern " penny dreadfuls," is less frequently presented for recitation.

I give this as an example, on the one hand, of a kind of poetry to be avoided—any poetry that appeals to the lower propensities, which are already far too potent for evil to require to be strengthened by the arts of the poet and the impress of genius. On the other hand, the pieces selected are often paltry in sentiment, and appeal to and rouse self-esteem and other emotions that are reprehensible in other directions, especially in some of our infant-room songs; though, one is delighted to observe, rapid improvement in these last.

The line of thought to be pursued by

teachers should be one that rigorously excludes all matter violating in any degree the training of our children in moral life, which ought to be as high and pure and ennobling as possible.

PIECES TO BE SELECTED.

But our aim in this direction should not only be the negative one of avoiding what is evil, but the positive one of selecting poems that will contribute to the moral development of the children entrusted to our care. The pieces should be gems for life, the best flowers in the wide and wonderful garden of English poesy, which our poets have so richly and sweetly produced—poems which our children will ever bless us to have learnt under our guidance, and which, in times of trial or temptation, that come to all, may strengthen the falling, and preserve the conscience from many a stain. This is surely a strain I need not further pursue, to create increased watchfulness among teachers, in the selection of the poetry their pupils commit to memory.

Happily, I am delighted to observe, in most cases, a rising perception of the importance of this subject of Recitation, and, in a lesser degree, of Reading, among our teachers, as valuable elements in moral training.

In selecting pieces, however, the moral element should not be obtruded as didactic moral teaching, which neither men nor children like much of; but the moral effects should be always present, and will prove the more powerful if they are produced rather than preached.*

2. PIECES FOR MUSIC. — The same principle should guide us in the selection of Songs to be sung in school. This should be done all the more carefully, because, in these, the charm of melody has been wedded

---

* Among those of a good type which I have had presented for Recitation and Meaning may be mentioned: Charles Swain's "What is Noble?" Lowell's "Heritage," and "The Fatherland," Whittier's "The Problem," Caroline F. Orne's "Labour," beginning "Ho! ye who at the anvil toil," Burns' "A man's a man for a' that," "The Daisy" of Chaucer and Burns, Charles Mackay's "There's a good time coming, boys," "Better than gold," "Dare to do right," "The power of gentleness," "Drive the nail aright," and many more of high tone.

L

to the potency of poetry. The pieces should be such as do not, on the one side, violate propriety or purity; and, on the other, have direct and active moral impulse.

CONVIVIAL SONGS TO BE AVOIDED.

Judged by this standard, for instance, that clever biographical song, with its fetching air, one of the most popular of the Scotch national bard's, "There was a lad was born in Kyle," will not bear criticism. You may be surprised that a lover, like myself, of Scotch poetry in general, and of Burns in particular, should object to such a poem. For children, I not only object to it, but protest against its use in schools. Is it desirable, is it right, is it conducive to the higher path along which we would guide the tottering feet of our little ones, that they should be asked to sing, in rousing chorus, about "Rantin' rovin' Robin"?

I am far from being any high and dry puritan in such matters. The song is splendid in special circumstances, but only for older folk, who can understand and appreciate its beauty and exquisite humour, and who know that the poet was even doing himself injustice by proclaiming that he was the "rantin' and rovin'" boy here described. But that is a very different thing from asking our children to sing, in their tender years, about "rantin' and rovin'." Is that not so? Is the subject not more serious than teachers have generally esteemed it? A like objection may be taken to many others, such as "Willie brewed a peck o' maut," to which young children are prematurely, and, I would add, perniciously, introduced even in school. The galaxy of Scottish and English Song has a thousand stars, as bright and pure as ever sparkled in the heavenly hyaline, without our having to choose such earthly glow-worms as these.

LOVE SONGS OBJECTIONABLE.

One word on another class of songs that should be avoided in our schools, and all the more carefully in the upper classes, when our children enter their teens and new impulses begin unconsciously to waken in their constitution—Love Songs, even if delicate in sentiment and winsome in melody. When used at all, these require to be selected with utmost caution, because they appeal, it is to be hoped, to emotions they have not experimentally felt.

Yet one sometimes hears Love Songs given in school, which the children cannot understand, as beyond their experience, and which therefore violate the principles of educational science; or which, if they do understand them, they should not have introduced to them during school life. I could mention many pieces thus unfit for school purposes, which are often sung in school; including such a mild example as "Ilka lassie has her laddie; ne'er a one ha'e I."

I need not further pursue the subject; but cannot dismiss it without earnestly drawing attention to possible abuses in this direction, to which custom or tradition, or want of consideration of all its relations, or all these together, have in no small degree blunted the perceptions of teachers and parents, who should be, not least in this seductive field, the guides and guardians of the minds and hearts of our children.

XII.—THE RELATION OF MORAL TRAINING TO RELIGIOUS INSTRUCTION.

But we have heard not unfrequently more than echoes—loud clamours—that such Moral teaching and training are, somehow and somewhere, antagonistic to Religion. If it is, so much the worse for the religion to which it is said to be antagonistic. The cry, where it is made, is at once narrow and senseless. Strangely and inexplicably, Moral teaching, apart from Creed-conning, would seem to be viewed by some earnest men with latent if not active suspicion, as, in some unknown way, antipathetic or harmful to Godliness and True Religion. Infinitely otherwise, it is Religion's chiefest friend, its best assistance, an intimate and essential portion of its life and mission; systematising that part of the wide religious field which deals with our work in daily life, and shedding on it all the light and interest and attractiveness it can cull from all sources at its command; pointing out the duties we ought to perform in all the daily relations of life, which duties should be performed with all the impulse and emotion of religious principle. The words "Religion in Common Life," which briefly and happily epitomise all moral training and instruction, put their nature and purpose in one phrase, and should attract the most apprehensive to their systematic and regular treatment in school.

"To consider it a religious duty to study these questions," as William Ellis well says, "with the intention of regulating conduct by the convictions formed, is a great step towards religious excellence."

THE GENERAL TEACHING OF MORAL DUTY IS SURELY NOW NEAR AT HAND.

So pure, so high, so entirely productive of truest gain in the priceless riches of life, so capable of lifting our future men and women from sad ignorance of their duties in daily life — ignorance for which their educators are culpably responsible—is this vital part of Education, that it is to be hoped not many years will pass before we shall see it daily and systematically taught in all our schools. If *we* are not wise or religious enough to do it, our posterity will, with surprise and indignation at our disastrous delay.

"Public Schools," as once more and finally pleaded for and prophesied by Ruskin, "in which the aim was to form character faithfully, would return the children in due time to their parents, worth more than their weight in gold."

THE END.

Printed by BALLANTYNE, HANSON & CO
Edinburgh and London

www.ingramcontent.com/pod-product-compliance
Lightning Source LLC
Chambersburg PA
CBHW032151160426
43197CB00008B/869